**APPLICATION
OF NUMBER**

CORE SKILLS

Maths for work:
Intermediate

The School Mathematics Project

CAMBRIDGE
UNIVERSITY PRESS

Published by the Press Syndicate of the University of Cambridge
The Pitt Building, Trumpington Street, Cambridge CB2 1RP
40 West 20th Street, New York, NY 10011–4211, USA
10 Stamford Road, Oakleigh, Melbourne 3166, Australia

© Cambridge University Press 1996

First published 1996

Printed in Great Britain by Scotprint Ltd, Musselburgh, Scotland

Designed and produced by Gecko Ltd, Bicester, Oxon

A catalogue record for this book is available from the British Library

Main authors	Andy Hall
	Ron Haydock
	Alan Knighton
	Paul Roder
	With contributions from
	Stan Dolan
Team leader	Paul Roder

The publishers would like to thank the following for supplying photographs:
page 9 – Bubbles/J. Woodcock
page 11 – Chessington World of Adventures
page 15 – Barnaby's Picture Library/Sheila Halsall
page 18 – J. Allan Cash Ltd./Cleland Rimmer
page 21 – English Heritage Photographic Library
page 24 – Steven Wooster/The Garden Picture Library
page 27 – Barnaby's Picture Library/MEL
page 29(l & r), 32, 35, 79 – Graham Portlock

ISBN 0 521 49817 1

Contents

To the student

As part of your GNVQ course you will need to complete a number of assignments in your chosen vocational area to demonstrate that you can apply numeracy skills. This book will help you to sharpen your numeracy techniques so that you can use them with confidence when they are needed.

There are four main sections, linked as shown below. On the next page is an index of core skills. If you know that you are going to need a particular skill, then look it up here. You can then decide whether to practise it in context by working through a case study or to look directly at the technique involved.

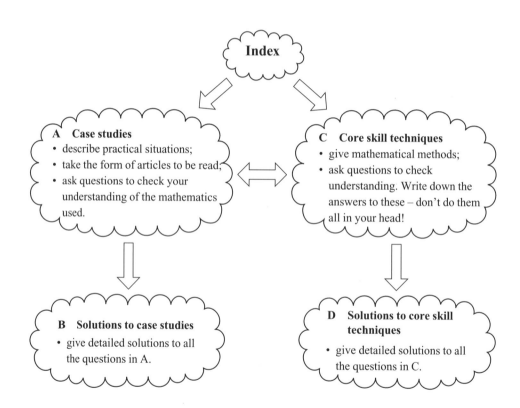

Index

A   Case studies
- describe practical situations;
- take the form of articles to be read;
- ask questions to check your understanding of the mathematics used.

C   Core skill techniques
- give mathematical methods;
- ask questions to check understanding. Write down the answers to these – don't do them all in your head!

B   Solutions to case studies
- give detailed solutions to all the questions in A.

D   Solutions to core skill techniques
- give detailed solutions to all the questions in C.

Index of GNVQ core skill techniques

Core skill techniques	1 Tin can labels	2 Food additives	3 Adventure park	4 Crisp boxes	5 Australia	6 The painter's problem	7 Landscaping	8 House prices	9 Relative business	10 Cycle computer	11 Planning permission	Page
1 Number												
Fractions, decimals, percentages and ratios	✓			✓		✓	✓			✓	✓	53
Probability descriptions							✓					59
Negative numbers									✓			60
Estimation, prediction and checking procedures	✓			✓					✓			61
Formulas in words and symbols				✓	✓					✓	✓	64
2 Shape, space and measure												
Units of measurement								✓				66
2-dimensional problems – perimeter and area	✓			✓		✓	✓		✓			68
3-dimensional problems – volumes	✓			✓							✓	71
Plans and drawings						✓	✓				✓	75
Measuring instruments and levels of accuracy							✓					77
3 Handling data												
Conversion of units					✓					✓		79
Data collection		✓	✓									82
Discrete and grouped data			✓									86
Mean, median, mode and range			✓						✓	✓		87
Graphs										✓		90
Pictograms, bar charts and pie charts			✓							✓		92

Case studies

1 Tin can labels

GNVQ core skill techniques:
- solving problems in two dimensions (perimeters and areas of plane shapes) (page 68);
- solving problems in three dimensions (volumes of cylinders) (page 71);
- calculating with decimals and percentages (page 54);
- using checking procedures (page 61).

Jill works in the sales department of a company which designs and manufactures labels. The company is contracted to supply labels for tins of baked beans. The diameter of each tin is 7 cm and the height is 10 cm.

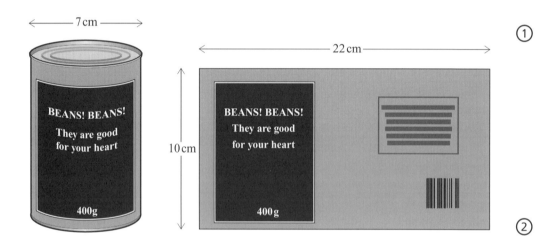

The minimum number of labels in an order is 500 and orders are always multiples of 500. In this case the contract is for 4500 labels.

The company charges these prices:

Area of label cm²	Price per 1000 £
150–174	£42
175–199	£44
200–224	£46
225–249	£48
250–274	£50
275–299	£52
300–324	£54
325–349	£56

Size of order	Discount
1–2000	0%
2001–5000	15%
5001–10 000	25%
10 001–50 000	35%
50 001–100 000	45%
100 000+	50%

Cost of 4500 labels
  @ £46 per thousand: £207.00   ④
Less 15% discount   £ 31.05 – ⑤
TOTAL   £175.95   ⑥

Jill works out the cost of 4500 labels to be £175·95 (or 3·91p per label). ③ She points out to the customer that if more than 10 000 labels are ordered then the cost per label is only 2·99p. The customer decides to increase the order to 11 000 labels. ⑦

Jill calculates that this will cost £328·90. ⑧

The customer also wants a smaller number of promotional labels advertising a '20% FREE' offer. 1500 of these labels are ordered.

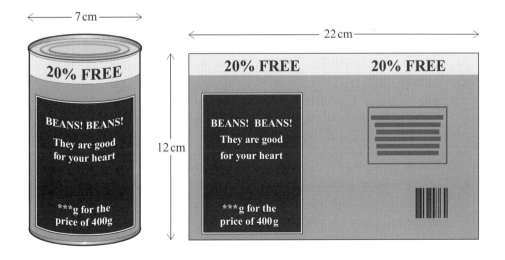

Jill calculates that this will cost £75. She points out that if they keep the height of the can the same (i.e. 10 cm) and increase the diameter to 7·7 cm, then there will still be a 20% increase in volume. However, the cost of the labels will only be £72.

⑨

⑩

Questions

1 (a) The customer decided to increase the order to 11 000 labels ⑦. Could he have increased the order to just 10 001 labels to obtain the cheaper rate?
 (b) What is the least number he could have increased his order to and still qualify for a 35% discount?

2 (a) Calculate the area of a standard label ①.
 (b) Explain why the length of a label was 22 cm if the diameter of the tin was 7 cm ①.

3 (a) '4500 labels @ £46 per thousand = £207' ④. How did Jill know that it should be £46 per thousand?
 (b) Explain how Jill calculated the cost as £75 ⑨.

4 (a) Calculate the volume of a tin can with height 10 cm and diameter 7 cm.
 (b) Calculate the volume of a tin can with height 10 cm and diameter 7·7 cm.
 (c) Check that the increase in volume is about 20% ⑩.
 (d) Calculate the area of the label for the bigger can and hence explain why Jill quoted a lower price for this shape of tin.

5 Explain how Jill calculated that the cost per label would be 3·91p ③.

6 (a) Jill could have checked her subtraction ⑤ by addition. What addition sum could she have done?
 (b) The customer was entitled to a 15% discount. Jill calculated that 15% of £207 is £31·05 ⑤. Was she right? Show how you calculate 15% of £207.
 (c) Jill knew that if you deduct 15% then you are left with 85%. She could have checked her total by calculating 85% of £207. Use this method to check the total ⑥.

7 (a) The promotional tin advertised 20% free. The original tin contained 400 g. How much would the promotional tin have contained?
 (b) Jill calculated that the cost of 11 000 labels was £328·90 ⑧. Write out a bill for 11 000 labels similar to the bill Jill wrote ④ and ⑤.

Solutions – page 38

2 Food additives

GNVQ core skill techniques:
- **designing and using a data collection procedure for a given sample (page 82);**
- **obtaining data from people (page 82).**

Additives cleared of driving kids wild

Despite widespread claims that food colouring and preservatives induce hyperactivity, research has revealed a very different picture ... After analysing questionnaires filled in by parents, researchers found that parents could not detect, purely from the children's behaviour, if they had taken the pill with the food colouring in it or the placebo (dummy pill).

Tony, an assistant on the research project described above, writes the following three questions to be included in the questionnaire:

(a) Did your son behave himself today?

(b) How many times did you smack your child today?

(c) How much more upset was your child after taking a pill?

In a pilot survey, he finds that parents have difficulty in answering the questions. Some unexpected responses are received which are extremely difficult to analyse; for example two responses to question (a) are:

- Yes, most of the time.
- Not really, but no worse than usual.

In the light of the replies, Tony rewrites the three questions so that it will be clear what type of response is expected. The new questions are:

(a) Was your child's behaviour generally: worse than normal?   ☐

the same as normal?   ☐

better than normal?   ☐

(b) (i) How many times did you punish your child for bad behaviour?   ☐

(ii) How many times did you reward or praise your child for good behaviour?   ☐

(c) (i) After taking the pill did his/her behaviour change?   Yes   ☐

No   ☐

(ii) If yes, was the change generally: better behaviour?   ☐

worse behaviour?   ☐

A total of 20 families take part in the pilot survey. They all agree to take part and are given a pill to be given to the child at the start of the day and a questionnaire to fill in at the end. A larger sample will be needed for the proper survey. Tony suggests that the questionnaires and pills be sent to 1000 families, but his team leader feels that a sample size of 200 will be sufficient. ⑥ ⑦

While Tony is waiting for the questionnaires to be returned he prepares an observation sheet to record the information as it arrives. His next job will be to analyse the data and, with the rest of the team, to interpret and draw conclusions.

Questions

1 What was wrong with the questions Tony included in the first questionnaire ① , ② and ③?

2 What was the purpose of the pilot survey ④?

3 Some unexpected responses to question (a) were received ⑤ . What type of responses do you think Tony was expecting?

4 Why was the questionnaire sent to a sample rather than the whole population ⑥?

5 Tony's suggested sample size of 1000 was reduced to 200 ⑦.
(a) Which sample size would give a more accurate picture of the population?
(b) Why do you think a sample size of 200 was used?

Solutions – page 39

3 Adventure park

GNVQ core skill techniques:
- **designing and using a data collection procedure for a given sample (page 82);**
- **obtaining data from written sources (page 82);**
- **obtaining data from people (page 82);**
- **working with discrete and grouped data (page 86);**
- **calculating mean and range (page 87);**
- **interpreting and constructing statistical diagrams (pictograms, bar charts and pie charts) (page 92).**

Three friends, Sarah, Maria and Zetta, decide to investigate Chessington World of Adventures for one of their college projects, so they send for an information pack.

They learn that the site of the World of Adventures originally housed a zoo, which, at its most popular, attracted over 800 000 visitors a year. In the early 1970s attendance figures began to decline and within a few years Chessington Zoo closed. After six years of planning and at a cost of £12 million the zoo was transformed into Chessington World of Adventures, opening in 1987.

The information pack also contains the following information.

Visitor numbers		Top eight most popular rides	
1987	0·84 million	1	The Vampire (V)
1988	1·15 million	2	Professor Burp's Bubbleworks (PBB)
1989	1·3 million	3	Dragon River (DR)
1990	1·5 million	4	Safari Skyway (SS)
1991	1·41 million	5	Runaway Minetrain (RM)
1992	1·17 million	6	Smugglers' Galleon (SG)
1993	1·5 million	7	Chessington Railroad (CR)
		8	Toytown Roundabout (TR)

①

Approximate staff numbers in 1993	Temporary	Permanent
Catering	130	30
Rides	100	20
Merchandising	65	8
Estates	50	20
Games	40	5
Front of house	50	0
Administration	0	40
Others	65	67

②

Sarah and Maria both decide to use bar graphs to represent the attendance figures.

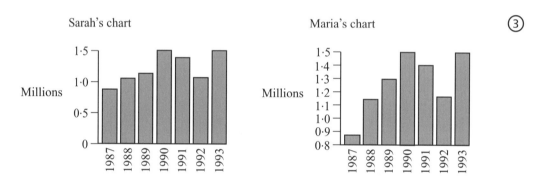

③

All three students also decide to represent the breakdown of staff numbers, but each of them chooses a different format.

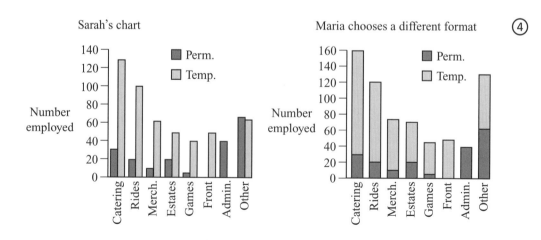

④

Zetta chooses to use pie charts. ⑤

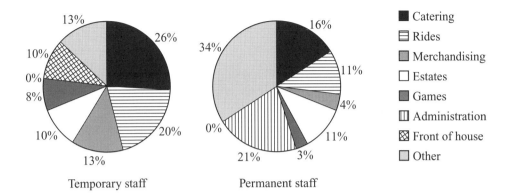

Legend	
■	Catering
☰	Rides
▨	Merchandising
☐	Estates
▨	Games
▥	Administration
⊠	Front of house
▢	Other

Temporary staff   Permanent staff

The three friends think that the information given in the information pack leaves many questions unanswered. They are particularly interested in the top eight rides – do girls prefer different rides to boys? What about the attendance – is the park equally popular with all age groups? They decide to investigate and set out for the park to collect their own data. Having designed an observation sheet, they decide that they will each survey a sample of 100 people selected at random in the park.

Observation sheet ⑥

Person	Favourite ride	Age	Gender
1	V	c	M
2	TR	d	F
3	V	c	
4	DR		

Age	
0–4	a
5–9	b
10–14	c
15–19	d
20–24	e
25+	f

They combine the three observation sheets and present the information they collect in tables.

Ride	Male	Female
The Vampire	53	30
Prof. Burp's Bubbleworks	18	31
Dragon River	15	17
Safari Skyway	9	9
Runaway Minetrain	18	14
Smugglers' Galleon	13	15
Chessington Railroad	2	8
Toytown Roundabout	6	18
Magic Carpet	6	6
Other	2	10

Age	Frequency	
0–4	29	⑦
5–9	66	
10–14	99	
15–19	36	
20–24	21	
25+	49	

They study the tables and discuss which statistical diagrams would be most useful to represent this information and help them draw conclusions.

Questions

1 (a) How many people had visited the World of Adventures up to 1993 ①?
   (b) What was the mean average annual attendance over the seven-year period?
   (c) Give the range of annual attendance figures from 1987 to 1993.

2 Sarah's and Maria's diagrams ③ both represent the same data. Which diagram represents the data best? Give a reason for your answer.

3 (a) How many more temporary than permanent staff were employed at the park ②?
   (b) Why do you think so many temporary staff were employed at the park?

4 Sarah and Maria both used bar charts to represent staffing ④ while Zetta decided to use pie charts ⑤. Look carefully at the diagrams and say what you think is good about each one.

5 Calculate the total number of temporary staff employed ② and use this to check that the percentages on Zetta's pie chart for temporary staff ⑤ are correct.

6 (a) When the students carried out the survey, why do you think they used codes to fill in the sheet ⑥?
   (b) Why do you think they decided to use groupings for age and why is there only a single group for over 25s ⑥?
   (c) What was the total size of the survey?

If available, use a computer package to draw the diagrams for questions 7, 8 and 9.

7 Display the information collected by the students on the popularity of the different rides ⑦ and comment on the results.

8 Use a pie chart to display the information on age collected by the students ⑦ and comment on the results.

9 Although pictograms only give simple representations of data, they are visually attractive. Design a pictogram to represent the popularity of rides, using the student's data ⑦.

Solutions – page 40

4 Crisp boxes

GNVQ core skill techniques:
- calculating using percentages (page 56);
- describing situations using percentages (page 56);
- calculating using simple formulas expressed in words (page 64);
- solving problems in two dimensions (area of rectangle) (page 68);
- solving problems in three dimensions (volume of cuboid) (page 71);
- interpreting and constructing 2-dimensional diagrams (page 71);
- interpreting and constructing 2-dimensional representations of 3-dimensional objects (page 72).

Every evening after school Sandip helps his father in his small supermarket. The shop is next door to a large comprehensive school and each day many packets of crisps are purchased. One of Sandip's tasks is to take the empty crisp boxes, pull them apart and lay them flat so that they do not take up much room and are easy to dispose of.

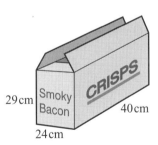

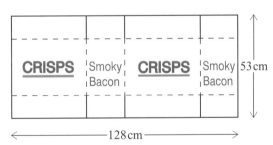

The design of the sheet of card seems very simple, but Sandip feels that a smaller sheet could be used to make a box big enough to hold the crisps. He measures the dimensions of the box and the sheet of card (to the nearest centimetre).

	Cardboard box	Cardboard sheet
Length (cm)	40	128
Width (cm)	24	53
Height (cm)	29	

He spots these relationships:
- The width of the sheet is equal to the width plus height of the box. ①
- The length of the sheet is twice the sum of the length and width of the box.

He calculates the volume of the box as $27\,840\,\text{cm}^3$ and the area of the sheet as ②
$6784\,\text{cm}^2$. Any further calculations will have to wait until after tea at home. ③

During tea Sandip discusses the problem with his grandfather, who dismisses the answer as obvious.

'The most compact shape is always the best, so use a cube.'

After tea Sandip checks his grandfather's solution. A 30 cm cube would have almost the same volume as the crisp box. (In fact the volume is $27\,000\,\text{cm}^3$, which is slightly less than the volume of the crisp box.)

If he were to use a 30 cm cube for the crisps then the sheet of cardboard used to make the box would have the dimensions:

$$\begin{aligned}
\text{width} &= \text{width of box} + \text{height of box} \\
&= (30 + 30)\,\text{cm} \\
&= 60\,\text{cm} \\
\text{length} &= \text{twice the sum of the length and width of the box} \\
&= 2 \times (30 + 30)\,\text{cm} \\
&= 120\,\text{cm}
\end{aligned}$$

and so the area of the sheet of card would be $7200\,\text{cm}^2$. ④

Compared with the actual box, this is more than 6% bigger! Grandfather can't believe the figures, so he checks the calculations.

$$\frac{7200 - 6784}{6784} \times 100\%$$

It's true; the cube is slightly smaller but nevertheless uses more cardboard.

'It's because the flaps overlap' he states. 'Go for a narrower, square box; that ⑤
should improve things.' Sandip says 'Yes, grandfather,' and quietly walks away shaking his head.

Questions

1 Sandip remembered that the nets of a cube were like this:

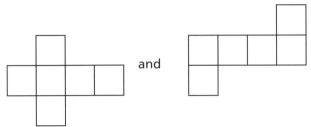

and

(a) How much cardboard would a net for a 30 cm cube use?
(b) Sketch a similar net for the $24 \times 29 \times 40$ cm crisp box.
(c) Which net uses the least cardboard?
(d) Explain why these nets are not practical designs.

2 For the crisp box, show that:
(a) the volume was 27 840 cm³ ② ;
(b) the area was 6784 cm² ③ .

3 (a) Show that the two relationships Sandip found were correct for the actual box ① .
(b) Explain why these relationships are true for all boxes made in this way.

4 Explain why the area was 7200 cm² ④ .

5 Grandad suggested a 'narrower, square box' ⑤ . The cardboard box shown fits this description:
(a) Calculate its volume.
(b) Sketch the sheet of cardboard used to make this box and calculate its area.
(c) Is this a better box? Give your reasons.

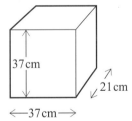

37 cm

21 cm

←—37 cm—→

6 Suppose the box in question 5 is on its side; that is, the height is 21 cm while the width and length are each 37 cm.
(a) Sketch the box and calculate its volume.
(b) Sketch the sheet of cardboard and calculate its area.
(c) Is this a better box? Give your reasons.

Solutions – page 42

5 Australia

GNVQ core skill techniques:
- calculating using simple formulas expressed in symbols (page 64);
- approximate calculations (page 61);
- converting between common units of measurement using scales and tables (page 79);
- converting between common units of measurement using calculations (page 81).

Clare has decided to visit her sister in Perth but she also wants to take the opportunity to see as much of Australia as possible.

Temperature in August (°C)		
	Max.	Min.
Alice Springs	26	10
Cairns	26	17
Darwin	31	21
Melbourne	15	7
Perth	18	9
Sydney	18	9

Alice Springs

910	**Cairns**				
820	1050	**Darwin**			
1230	1680	2050	**Melbourne**		
1240	2150	1760	1690	**Perth**	
1260	1240	2080	440	2050	**Sydney**

Distances (km)

After spending a week in Perth with her sister, she intends using internal flights to follow this itinerary:

Perth → Darwin → Cairns → Sydney → Alice Springs → Perth

She decides to go for four weeks and, being a teacher, she must go in August, our summer but their winter! In order to decide what clothes to take she looks up the temperatures which are given in the brochure. She is used to measuring air temperature in Fahrenheit (°F) but the brochure only gives temperatures in Celsius (°C). However, it does provide the following conversion scale.

She notes that on her trip the temperature could range from 50°F up to 90°F, so she decides to pack some warm clothes as well as T-shirts and shorts. ④

Clare is interested in just how far she will be travelling in Australia and uses the brochure to look up the distances. She finds that she will cover 6550 km! But what is this in miles? Again, the ⑤ brochure gives the conversion but this time in the form of a table.

km	10	20	30	40	50	60	70	80	90	100
miles	6	12	19	25	31	37	43	50	56	62

⑥

km	100	200	300	400	500	600	700	800	900	1000
miles	62	124	186	249	311	373	435	497	559	621

As 1000 km = 621 miles, she works out that her total journey in miles is $6 \cdot 55 \times 621$. She estimates this as $7 \times 600 = 4200$ miles. (She does an accurate ⑦ calculation later.)

Australia's vast open spaces make air travel the natural way to journey between cities and tourist areas. Clare discovers that she can travel at a special fare, available only to tourists, by buying coupons in this country at £100 each and ⑧ then using one coupon for each domestic flight within Australia. She is not convinced this is the cheapest method and so she asks her sister to find out the local prices of flights.

Route	Price in Australian dollars ($)
Perth to Darwin	$ 260
Darwin to Cairns	$ 200
Cairns to Sydney	$ 125
Sydney to Alice Springs	$ 178
Alice Springs to Perth	$ 216

From her bank, Clare finds the exchange rate to be 2·13 Australian dollars to the pound. (She works out that this means one Australian dollar is worth about 47p.) She calculates the price of internal flights in pounds and decides to ask her sister to book the tickets.

⑨
⑩
⑪

Questions

1 Trace the map of Australia ① and draw Clare's route ③.

2 (a) Explain how Clare found what the temperature range for her trip was likely to be ④.
   (b) From school Clare remembered the formula $F = \frac{9}{5}C + 32$ to convert from °C to °F.
   Use this formula to copy and convert the 'Temperature in August' table ② to degrees Fahrenheit and check Clare's temperature range ④.

3 (a) Use the distance chart ② to find the distance (in km) between:
   (i) Perth and Darwin   (ii) Cairns and Sydney.
   (b) 'Clare found that she would cover 6550 km' ⑤. Explain how she worked this out.

4 (a) Use the conversion table ⑥ to convert the distance between Perth and Darwin to miles.
   (b) Convert each stage of Clare's route to miles and put these figures on the map you drew in question 1.
   (c) Is 4200 miles ⑦ an over-estimate or an under-estimate?

5 (a) What would be the total cost of Clare's internal flights if she used the coupons ⑧ and booked the flights in this country?
   (b) How did Clare convert the exchange rate from $2·13 = £1 to $1 = 47p ⑩?
   (c) Use the exchange rate ⑨ to find the cost (in pounds) from Perth to Darwin of a local booking.
   (d) Why did Clare ask her sister to book the tickets ⑪? Show all your working to support your explanation.

6 The return flight from England to Australia is £897. Using the exchange rate of $2·13 to the pound, find the cost of the flight in dollars.

Solutions – page 44

6 The painter's problem

GNVQ core skill techniques:
- calculating with fractions and ratios (page 53);
- solving problems in two dimensions (perimeter and area) (page 68);
- interpreting and constructing 2-dimensional diagrams (page 75).

Andrew is a painter and decorator specialising in older properties. A customer asks him to decorate a room in an 18th century house. The owner has discovered a small section of the original paint and would like Andrew to paint the walls of the room in a colour as near as possible to the original.

The colour appears to be a mixture of a red and a blue so he decides to experiment by mixing red and blue until he finds a good match.
He starts off with a mixture of one part red to one part blue. He paints a small part of the wall with this mixture and labels it 1 : 1.

①

This looks rather red so he mixes one part red to two parts blue, paints another section of wall and labels it 1 : 2.

②

This still looks rather red, so he tries a 1 : 3 (i.e. one to three) mixture. However, this looks too blue, so he decides to try a mixture between 1 : 2 and 1 : 3.

He knows that 1 : 3 is the same as 2 : 6,

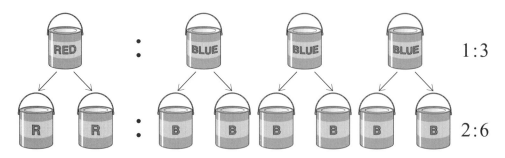

and that 1 : 2 is the same as 2:4,

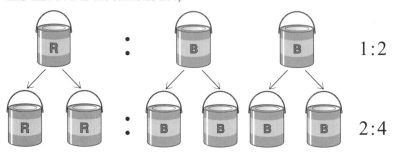

so he decides to try a 2 : 5 mixture. This seems a perfect match. He shows the customer the section of wall painted with the two to five mixture and the customer agrees that it is close enough to the original.

③

He now has to estimate how much paint he will need. He measures the room and calculates the perimeter to be 20 metres.

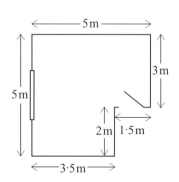

④

As the walls of the room are 2·5 m high, he calculates that the area to be painted is approximately 50 m². (This is, of course, a slight over-estimate as no deduction has been made for the door and window, but he knows from experience that it is better to mix too much paint than to discover later there is not enough to complete the

⑤

room.) The walls will need two coats of paint and he knows that 1 litre of paint will cover about $12\,m^2$ of wall, so he calculates that he will need 8·33 litres of paint.　⑥

With a 2 : 5 mixture, $\frac{2}{7}$ of the paint should be red and $\frac{5}{7}$ should be blue.　⑦

He needs $8\cdot33 \div 7 \times 2 = 2\cdot38$ litres of the red and 5·95 litres of the blue.　⑧

Paint comes in 1 litre, $2\frac{1}{2}$ litre and 5 litre tins, so Andrew will need a $2\frac{1}{2}$ litre tin of red paint, and a 1 litre tin and a 5 litre tin of the blue.

Questions

1　(a) Andrew tried a 1 : 1 mixture ①. What fraction of the mixture was red paint?

　　(b) Then he tried a 1 : 2 mixture ②. What fraction of this mixture was blue paint?

　　(c) Explain why in a 2 : 5 mixture, $\frac{2}{7}$ of the mixture is red ⑦.

2　Andrew finally chose a 2 : 5 mixture ③. If he used a 1 litre tin of red paint, how much blue paint would he need to make the mixture?

3　Would a 3 : 7 mixture have too much or too little red paint in it? Explain your answer.

4　Check that the perimeter of the room was 20 m ④.

5　Explain how Andrew calculated the area of the room to be $50\,m^2$ ⑤.

6　Andrew calculated that he would need 8·33 litres of paint ⑥. Explain how he arrived at this figure.

7　Andrew calculated that he would need 5·95 litres of blue paint to decorate the room ⑧. Explain carefully how you think he calculated this.

Solutions – page 46

7 Landscaping

GNVQ core skill techniques:
- calculating with percentages (page 56);
- calculating using common units (page 66);
- solving problems in two dimensions (areas of plane shapes) (page 68);
- interpreting and constructing 2-dimensional diagrams (page 75);
- choosing and using appropriate measuring instruments and appropriate units of measurement for the task (page 77);
- choosing and working within appropriate tolerances for a measuring task (page 77);
- choosing and using an appropriate level of accuracy for a measuring task (page 77).

Paul is a landscape gardener. A customer asks him to quote for a job, so he visits the site and makes a few notes. There is a belt of trees behind a house and behind this there is a rough patch of ground which needs landscaping. The customer wants a large part levelled and turf laid to create a lawn. To the side of this he wants Paul to create a wild flower area. Paul has to supply the turf and the wild flower seed.

He always orders turf from an old established firm near Colchester. Their turf cutting machinery is set to cut turfs which measure 81 inches by 16 inches.

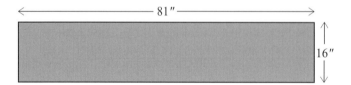

①

This is precisely 1 yd^2 (square yard), so it is appropriate to measure the dimensions of the proposed lawn in yards rather than metres. The wild flower seed supplier, on the other hand, recommends 50 grams of wild flower seed is scattered on each square metre, so in this case it is appropriate to use metres to measure the wild flower area.

Paul uses a long tape-measure which is graduated in both metric and imperial units so that he can use the units which are most appropriate for the job. He takes some measurements and draws a rough sketch of the site.

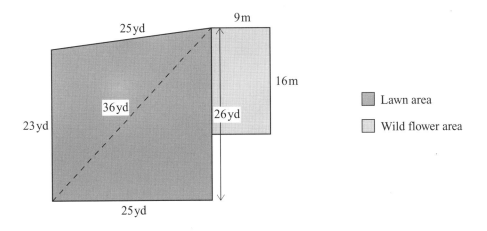

When he gets home he calculates how much the job is worth. The turf is expensive, so first calculates the lawn area. This area is not a straightforward shape like a simple rectangle, so he starts off by making a scale drawing on his drawing-board. He chooses a scale of 1 cm to 1 yard as the resulting drawing will be big enough for him to take accurate measurements but not too big to fit on his drawing-board.

The lawn area can be divided up into two triangles. One is a simple right-angled triangle and its area is easy to calculate. He measures the height of the other triangle from his scale drawing so that he can calculate the area of this triangle as well. His measurements are shown on the sketch below.

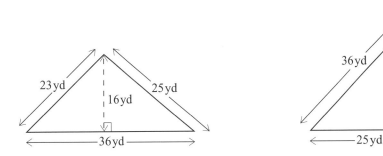

② ③ ④ ⑤ ⑥

He calculates that the areas of the triangles are 325 yd^2 and 288 yd^2. He will therefore need to order 613 turfs. As they are sold in tens he decides to round this up to 620.

The wild flower area is approximately 144 m^2 so he will need 7·2 kg of seed. This is sold in 2$\frac{1}{2}$ kg bags so he allows for 3 bags.

He works with his assistant, Mike, and estimates that it will take 4 days for the two of them to complete the job. The money he gets for the job must cover the running costs of any machinery he uses, wages for himself and Mike, as well as a profit for the business. As a rule of thumb he charges £250 per day. (If he charges too much then he may not get the contract.) He writes out a quote for the job on his company's notepaper and posts it to the customer.

GARDENING SERVICES AND LANDSCAPING

To clear, level and prepare area for turf. To lay turf. To clear, level and prepare area for seed. To sow seed. To clear away and dispose of all waste.

Labour:	£1000
Turf:	£ 651
Seed:	£ 45
SUB TOTAL	£1696
VAT (17.5%)	£296·80
TOTAL	£1992·80

⑦ ⑧

⑨

Questions

1 All Paul's measurements were rounded up to the next whole number. For example, if he measured a length as being 23·15 m, he rounded it up to 24 m even though it was nearer 23 m. Why do you think he chose to work to these tolerances?

2 He made a scale drawing of the lawn area ②. What measuring instruments do you think he used for this task and what level of accuracy do you think he worked to?

3 There are 36 inches in a yard so one square yard is a square measuring 36 in by 36 in. Show that a single turf ① had an area of 1 square yard.

4 (a) Show how he calculated the areas of the triangles to be 325 yd² and 288 yd² ③.
  (b) Check that he would need 613 turfs ④.

5 'The wild flower area is approximately 144 m² so he will need 7·2 kg of seed. This is sold in $2\frac{1}{2}$ kg bags so he allows for 3 bags' ⑤ and ⑥. Explain how Paul worked out these figures.

6 Paul allowed £651 for turf and £45 for wild flower seed ⑦ and ⑧. How much did each turf cost and how much was a bag of seed?

7 Check that Paul correctly calculated the subtotal, VAT and final total in the quote he sent to the customer ⑨.

Solutions – page 47

8 House prices

GNVQ core skill techniques:
- **using probability to describe situations (page 59);**
- **calculating and using mean, median, mode and range (page 87).**

Winston is an estate agent who carries out a regular analysis of houses the firm has sold in different areas of the city. He compares house sales over the previous two months for the districts of Portly and Ashfield.

Portly	
£ 68 000	2-bed. detached
£ 34 000	2-bed. flat
£ 95 000	4-bed. detached
£ 45 000	3-bed. semi
£ 82 000	3-bed. detached
£105 000	4-bed. detached
£ 84 000	3-bed. detached
£ 75 000	4-bed. semi
£ 87 000	3-bed. detached

Ashfield	
£460 000	6-bed. detached with outbuildings
£ 50 000	3-bed. semi
£ 48 000	3-bed. semi
£ 24 000	1-bed. flat
£ 31 000	2-bed. terraced
£ 44 000	3-bed. terraced
£ 65 000	3-bed. detached
£ 28 000	2-bed. maisonette
£ 24 000	1-bed. flat
£ 38 000	2-bed. terraced
£174 000	5-bed. detached
£ 70 000	3-bed. detached

①

He first notes the tremendous range of values for Ashfield: £436 000!

To make a simple comparison between the two districts he decides to average the sales figures for each district. He calculates that the average selling prices are £75 000 for Portly and £88 000 for Ashfield. For a further comparison he compares the prices of similar types of houses in the two districts.

②
③

A client with a 3-bedroomed detached house on an estate in Portly has a new job in a different part of the country and so would like a quick sale, but would, of course, like to get as much as possible for the property. Winston values her house at between £80 000 and £90 000. She asks him what the probability is of selling her house for, say, £87 000 within three months. Winston notes from his records

④
⑤

for the last year that of ten houses like hers just one sold for over £85 000 within three months, while four sold for between £80 000 and £85 000 within the same period. In reply to her enquiry he estimates the probability at 10%. She asks him to put her house on the market at £85 000, believing she has a 50% chance of selling it within three months if she is prepared to accept offers in the region of £82 000.

⑥

⑦

Questions

1   (a)   How did Winston arrive at the figure of £436 000 for the range of house sales in Ashfield ①?
    (b)   Find the range of selling prices in Portly.
    (c)   What conclusions can you draw from the range of selling prices in Ashfield and Portly?

2   What was the total value of property sold over the two-month period in:
    (a)   Portly,   (b)   Ashfield?

3   (a)   Winston referred to 'average selling price' ②. Which average – mean, median or mode – do you think he used?
    (b)   Check his figures of £75 000 and £88 000 ③.

4   (a)   When he compared the mean selling price, was Winston correct to assume that Ashfield was the more affluent district?
    (b)   He went on to compare similar types of houses in the two districts ③. How was this comparison likely to affect his view of the two districts?
    (c)   Find the median and modal selling price for each district.
    (d)   Which average, mean, median or mode, do you think gave the best comparison between the selling prices in the two districts? Give your reasons.

5   (a)   Why do you think Winston valued the house at between £80 000 and £90 000 ④?
    (b)   For how much do you think Winston would have valued a similar house (i.e. 3-bedroomed detached) in Ashfield?

6   How did Winston arrive at the figure of 10% ⑥ for the probability of selling the house within three months?

7   From Winston's figures ⑤, would you agree with the client's view that she had a 50% probability of selling her house within three months if she was prepared to accept offers in the region of £82 000 ⑦? Give reasons to support your answer.

Solutions – page 48

9 Relative business

GNVQ core skill techniques:
- **using negative numbers in calculations and in describing situations (page 60);**
- **using estimation to predict outcomes (page 61);**
- **calculating and using mean and range (page 87);**
- **interpreting and constructing line graphs (page 90);**
- **selecting and using appropriate axes, scales and labels (page 90);**
- **interpreting statistical diagrams (bar charts) (page 92).**

Marita and Dara are cousins who started up in business at the same time, five years ago. Marita is cautious but energetic and she doesn't mind getting up early! She runs the newspaper shop which she took over from her father, with occasional help from him and a team of delivery boys and girls. Dara is the entrepreneurial type, ready to take a risk. She decided to capitalise on her knowledge of electronics and set up as a supplier of electronic communications equipment. Her parents promised to subsidise her for a while until the business got off the ground. Marita and Dara meet to compare notes on their first five years.

> **Marita:** Business is nice and steady. I took over a going concern with plenty of regular customers and I pick up a few more each year. My expenses are predictable – the rent for the shop, the girls' and boys' wages and my dad's money. I do my own cleaning and keep the books.

This year Marita makes a net return on sales of £42 750, out of which she pays an average of £1050 per month in wages and expenses and £560 per month in rent. This means that she makes an overall profit of £23 430, which she keeps as her salary. ①

Marita's five-year results (overall profit)

Year	1	2	3	4	5
Profit (£)	17 110	19 580	19 470	21 660	23 430

Marita calculates her total profit as £101 250 and her mean annual profit as £20 250, with a range of £6320.

②

Bar chart showing Marita's profit over five years

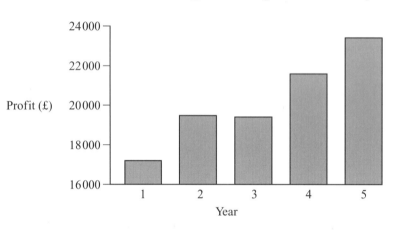

Dara: At first I had terrific expenses. The rent isn't too high but the premises had to be improved and equipped and there was the cost of the stock. So I was in the red for a couple of years. But the market's huge; trade has built up fast and should continue to boom. After two years I broke even and now I've reached the stage when I'm paying Dad and Mum back what I've borrowed.

This year Dara makes a net return on sales of £35 210. Her rent is £350 per month, and expenses, including the wages of a cleaner and stores keeper, have averaged £905 a month. So her overall profit is £20 150, out of which she takes her salary and starts to repay her parents.

③

Dara's five-year results (overall profit)

Year	1	2	3	4	5
Profit (£)	⁻5110	⁻3330	760	9580	20 150

④

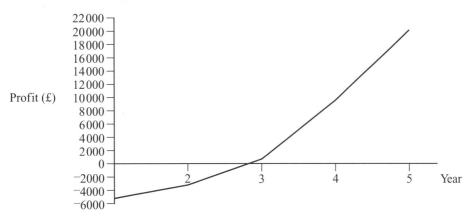

Line graph showing Dara's profit over five years

The two cousins agree that keeping track of each other's progress is very interesting and decide that they will have another 'business meeting' in two years' time. ⑤

Questions

1 Show how the cousins calculated their overall profit ① and ③.

2 Show how Marita's mean profit and range were calculated ②.

3 Use the same method to find the mean and range of annual profits for Dara ④.

4 Give two reasons for the large difference between the ranges for Marita and Dara.

5 How was a loss shown:
   (a) in Dara's table of profits,   (b) in the line graph?

6 Draw line graphs on the same set of axes to show Marita's and Dara's profits over the five-year period.

The next question has no 'correct' answer but you should be able to make an 'educated guess'. See how this compares with the solution given.

7 Dara was thinking of her 'business meeting' with Marita in two years' time ⑤. She thought: 'the way business is going, my mean profit over the first seven years will be more than Marita's'.
   (a) Use the graph you drew in question 6 to predict the profits for the next two years for both businesses.
   (b) Do you agree that Dara was right? Justify your answer.

Solutions – page 50

10 Cycle computer

GNVQ core skill techniques:
- **calculating with decimals (page 54);**
- **calculating using simple formulas (page 64);**
- **solving problems in two dimensions (perimeter of circle) (page 69);**
- **converting between common units of measurements using calculations (page 81).**

An electronic cycle computer measures the distance you travel and your speed. It comes in three parts:

- a magnet,
- a sensor,
- a processing and display unit.

The magnet is fastened on to a spoke of the front wheel and the sensor is attached to the front fork to count each time the magnet passes it. This information is conveyed electrically to the third unit, which is fixed to the handlebar. The unit converts revolutions to distance and also, using its in-built clock, to speed. Distance and speed are displayed where they can be easily seen.

When you fit the computer you have to set it for your wheel size so that at each turn it will add a distance equal to the circumference of the wheel. The instructions tell you to find the circumference:

either by rolling the bike along level ground,

or by measuring the diameter and multiplying by 3·14.

For example, if you find the diameter is 661 mm, then the circumference is
661 × 3·14 = 2076 mm (to the nearest mm).

①

The number used to set the computer is found by dividing the circumference in
millimetres by 10. This input number must be whole, so in the case of the wheel
with diameter 661 mm you would calculate:

$$2076 \div 10 = 207{\cdot}6$$
$$= 208 \quad \text{(to the nearest whole number)}$$

and you would input this number 208. Two further examples are shown in this
table.

Circumference in mm	Input number
Between 2255 and 2264	226
Between 2095 and 2104	210

Tasmin has been given the job of rewriting the instructions of the German
manufacturers for United States consumers, who prefer their distances in miles
and their speeds in miles per hour (m.p.h.).

She knows that a mile is 1·61 km, so in her first attempt she describes how to
measure the circumference in millimetres, then puts in another step, dividing by
1·61, before finally dividing by 10 to find the input number. She gives an
example:

②

③

Circumference in mm	2089
Divide by 1·61	1298
Divide by 10	129·8 = 130 (to the nearest whole number)

④

She tells the users that after inputting a number found in this way their computer
will register speeds in m.p.h. and distances in miles.

At this stage, Tasmin realises that her instructions are not very user-friendly. In a
second draft of her rewrite she decides to avoid metric measurements altogether.
From an encyclopedia she finds that 1 inch = 25·4 mm, so she makes out her
instructions as follows:

   A   Measure wheel diameter in inches, to nearest tenth.

⑤

   B   Multiply by 3·14.

   C   Multiply by 25·4.

   D   Divide by 1·61.

   E   Divide by 10.

Finally she realises that instructions B–E can be replaced by a single multiplication. Her final instructions read:

    A   Measure wheel diameter in inches, to nearest tenth. ⑥

    B   Multiply by 4·95.

Questions

1   The number 3·14 is an approximation to π. Use your calculator to compare $3\!\cdot\!14 \times 661$ and $\pi \times 661$ ①. Is the output number affected?

2   (a) Suppose that the speedometer was set to show m.p.h. If the bike was travelling at 15 km/hour what would the speedo show ②?
     (b) Why did Tasmin have to *divide* by 1·61 rather than multiply ③?

3   A child's bike has a front wheel diameter of 386 mm. Find:
     (a) its circumference,
     (b) the input number for km readings,
     (c) the input number for mile readings.

4   Suppose that users were asked to measure the *circumference* rather than the diameter ⑥. Complete these instructions to find the input number.

    A   Measure circumference in inches, to nearest tenth.

    B   Multiply by (?).

5   In her first draft ③, Tasmin could have quoted the formula:

$$n = \frac{C}{16\cdot1}$$

   where n is the input number and C is the circumference in millimetres.
     (a) Show that this formula gives the same input number of 130 ④.
     (b) Find n if $C = 2110$.

6   (a) Use Tasmin's instructions A–E in her second draft ⑤ to find the input number if the wheel diameter is 24·8 inches.
     (b) Now use her simpler instructions A and B in her final draft ⑥ and check that you get the same answer.
     (c) Why do the two methods give the same answer?

Solutions – page 51

11 Planning permission

GNVQ core skill techniques:
- calculating with percentages (page 56);
- calculating using simple formulas expressed in words (page 64);
- solving problems in three dimensions (volumes of simple shapes) (page 71);
- interpreting and constructing 2-dimensional diagrams (plans) (page 75);
- interpreting and constructing 2-dimensional representations of 3-dimensional objects (page 71).

Simon is a builder based in Bury St Edmunds in Suffolk. He specialises in building extensions, and as part of the service he provides he draws up detailed plans of a proposed extension for submission to the local planning authority. A customer asks Simon to quote for an extension. The customer lives in an unusual house in one of the villages near Bury St Edmunds. The house is unusual because it is round.

The house is about 120 years old and built of local flint and brick. The customer wishes to extend her house using materials as close to the original as possible. The proposed extension is quite modest and will not be visible from the road. Even so, Simon is not sure if planning permission is needed. The rules on planning change from time to time so Simon phones the planning office. He is told that:
- for any extension, the plans have to be sent to the local planning authority to be passed by the building inspector;
- if the volume of the proposed extension is more than 15% of the volume of the original house, then planning permission is needed.

If planning permission is needed then the plans have to be approved by the council planning committee. Simon has no doubt that the plans would be approved by the committee, but planning permission costs money and takes time so it is a good idea to find out if it is necessary.

First he calculates the volume of the original house. It is basically a cylinder with a cone on the top.

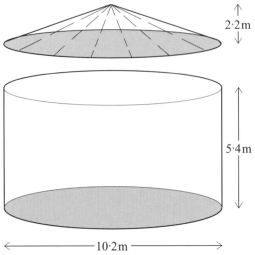

He looks up the appropriate formulas.

Volume of cylinder = base area × height   ①
$$= 441 \cdot 25 \, m^3$$

Volume of cone = base area × height ÷ 3   ②
$$= 59 \cdot 92 \, m^3$$

The total volume of the house is therefore $501 \cdot 17 \, m^3$. Simon now knows that, so   ③
long as the volume of the extension is less than $75 \cdot 18 \, m^3$, planning permission   ④
will not be necessary.

The outline plans for the extension are shown below.

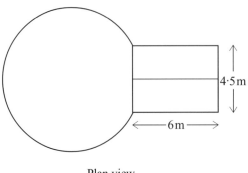

Plan view

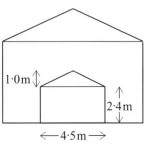

⑤

Side view

The extension is basically a cuboid
with a triangular prism on top.

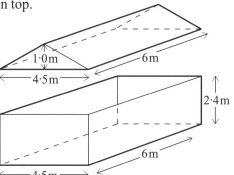

⑥

Simon calculates the volume using the fomulas:

volume of cuboid = length × width × height ⑦
= 64·8 m³

volume of triangular prism = area of triangle × length of prism ⑧
= 13·5 m³

so the total volume of the proposed extension is 78·3 m³. As this is greater than ⑨
75·16 m³ the customer will have to apply for planning permission.

Questions

1   Show the calculations Simon did when he worked out:
    (a) the volume of the cylinder ①,
    (b) the volume of the cone ②,
    (c) the total volume of the house ③,
    (d) the volume of the cuboid ⑦,
    (e) the volume of the triangular prism ⑧,
    (f) the total volume of the extension ⑨.

2   Explain how Simon calculated the value 75·18 m³ ④.

3   The customer preferred to start the job as soon as possible and not wait
    for planning permission. She suggested to Simon that the length of the
    extension (6 m shown in ⑤ and ⑥) could be reduced to 5·76 m. Was
    her calculation correct? Would the volume of the extension now be less
    than 75·18 m³? Show your calculation.

4   *Sketch* the house with its extension.

Solutions – page 52

B Solutions (Case studies)

1 Tin can labels

1 (a) No. The order had to be a multiple of 500 (i.e. 500, 1000, 1500, 2000, …).
   (b) 10 500

2 (a) Area of rectangle = length × width
                      $= 22 \times 10$
                      $= 220 \, \text{cm}^2$

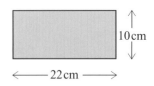

   (b) The length of the rectangle has to wrap around the circle of the tin so its length must be the circumference of a circle with diameter 7 cm.

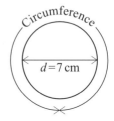

   $$c = \pi \times d$$
   $$= \pi \times 7$$
   $$= 21 \cdot 991\,14\ldots \text{ cm}$$
   $$= 22 \text{ cm (to the nearest mm)}$$

3 (a) The area of the label was 220 cm². Jill looked up the price in the table:

Area of label (cm²)	Price per 1000
200–224	£46

   (b) The area of the label was $12 \times 22 = 264 \, \text{cm}^2$.
        Any label with area between 250 and 274 cm² would cost £50 per thousand, so 1500 labels would cost $1 \cdot 5 \times 50 = £75$.

4 (a) Volume $= \pi r^2 h$
             $= \pi \times 3 \cdot 5 \times 3 \cdot 5 \times 10$
             $= 385 \, \text{cm}^3$ (to nearest cm³)
   (b) Volume $= \pi r^2 h$
             $= \pi \times 3 \cdot 85 \times 3 \cdot 85 \times 10$
             $= 466 \, \text{cm}^3$ (to nearest cm³)
   (c) Increase = 81 cm³ ⇒ fraction increase $= \frac{81}{385}$
                                     $= 0 \cdot 2103\ldots$
                                     $= 21\%$ (to nearest %)
        (The increase was just over 20% so the new can would be large enough to contain a 20% increase.)
   (d) Circumference of wider tin was $\pi \times 7 \cdot 7 = 24 \cdot 2$ cm. So area of label was $24 \cdot 2 \times 10 = 242 \, \text{cm}^2$. This size label is in the range 225–249 cm² and costs £48 per 1000 so price for 1500 labels was $1 \cdot 5 \times 48 = £72$.

5   It cost £175·95 for 4500 labels, so one cost 175·95 ÷ 4500 = £0·0391
$$= 3·91p$$

6   (a)   175·95 + 31·05 = 207·00
    (b)   15% of £207 = 0·15 × 207
$$= £31·05$$
    (c)   85% of £207 = 0·85 × 207
$$= £175·95$$

7   (a)   20% of 400 g = 0·2 × 400
$$= 80 g$$
    so the promotional tin contained 400 g + 20% = 400 + 80
$$= 480 g$$

   (b)   11 000 labels @ £46 per thousand   £506·00
         less 35% discount   £177·10 −
         Total   £328·90

2 Food additives

1   Question (a) is rather vague; a number of parents may have found it difficult to answer, resulting in many different responses. Also, the question assumes that the child is a boy.
Question (b) may result in misleading data. It is easy to make assumptions when writing questions for inclusion on a questionnaire. An answer of zero here could mean that the child had been well behaved, or that the parent did not believe in smacking. For some parents the question may be rather sensitive.
Question (c) is a leading question. It suggests that the child was in fact more upset.

2   Once a survey has been completed it is too late to go back and change questions that do not give the required data. A pilot survey is normally carried out on a small number of people to show up any likely problems before the main survey is undertaken.

3   'Yes' or 'no'!

4   You could not possibly try out an experiment on food additives on every child or teenager in the country; it would be unmanageable, besides being too expensive and time-consuming. You would need to choose a sample of children to take part and from their results make deductions about the whole population of children.

5   (a) A sample size of 1000
    (b) A sample size of 1000 would be too expensive.
         In this case the people were selected beforehand and agreed to take
         part in the experiment, hence a good return of questionnaires could be
         expected. However, the response to postal returns is usually poor.
         A sample size of 200 is a relatively small number. The people taking
         part would need to be chosen very carefully to ensure that they were
         representative of the whole population.

3 Adventure park

1   (a) $0·84 + 1·15 + 1·3 + 1·5 + 1·41 + 1·17 + 1·5 = 8·87$ million
    (b) $8·87 ÷ 7 = 1·27$ million
    (c) 0·84 million to 1·5 million, a range of 0·66 million or 660 000

2   On Sarah's diagram the frequency scale starts at 0 but on Maria's diagram it
    starts at 800 000 (0·80 million). As a result, Maria's diagram seems to
    indicate a large variation in attendance figures. Sarah's diagram is a better
    representation of the overall picture of attendance figures, showing a gradual
    increase through the first few years of reopening and then levelling off.
    Maria's diagram may be used by the publicity department of the park to
    indicate a large increase of attendance!

3   (a) Temporary staff: 500   Permanent staff: 190
         There were 310 more temporary than permanent staff.
    (b) The park is only open to the public during the summer so the majority
         of jobs will offer seasonal employment only, with a smaller number of
         staff employed through the year on a permanent basis.

4   Sarah's chart highlights the differences between permanent and temporary
    staff while Maria's highlights the total number of employees in each job.
    Zetta's pie charts highlight the different distribution of jobs comparing
    temporary with permanent employees. However, note that the pie chart gives
    no indication that there are many more temporary employees than permanent.

5   Number of temporary staff $= 500$
    Catering: $\frac{130}{500} \times 100 = 26\%$ Rides: $\frac{100}{500} \times 100 = 20\%$
    Merchandising: $\frac{65}{500} \times 100 = 13\%$ and so on.

6   (a) To save time.
    (b) The data would be much easier to analyse in grouped form. Age could be a
         sensitive issue – age groupings would help to get over this possible problem.
         They only had a single group for the 25s and over because they probably

felt that adventure parks would be more likely to appeal to younger people so they would be unlikely to sample many people aged 25 and over.

(c) 300

7

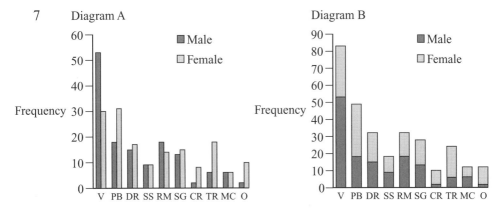

Diagram B indicates that on this survey the Safari Skyway and Chessington Railroad were less popular than the official figures indicate. This may have been due to the particular day on which the survey was taken (a school day with a lot of school trips and few families!). Otherwise, the survey agrees very closely with the information supplied by Chessington World of Adventures.

Diagram A gives a more detailed breakdown according to gender and does indicate that whereas the Vampire was by far the most popular ride among boys, this was not the case for girls where Professor Burp's Bubbleworks was equally popular. The diagram certainly indicates that males and females had different preferences and these may need to be taken into account when planning new rides.

8 Pie chart to show attendance according to age:

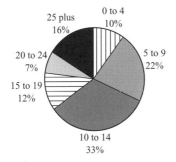

The survey indicated that the park was most popular amongst 10- to 14-year-olds, closely followed by the 5- to 9-year-olds. The survey may have been influenced by the day on which it was carried out. If the survey had been carried on a school day, school trips (primary and secondary) could have affected the results. Weekend figures could be quite different!

9 Pictogram showing the popularity of rides.

4 Crisp boxes

1 (a) There are 6 sides each with area $30 \times 30 = 900 \text{ cm}^2$.
Total area: $6 \times 900 = 5400 \text{ cm}^2$.

   (b)

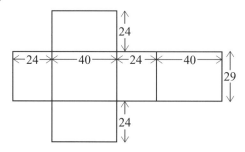

   (c) Area of crispbox:
2 sides at $24 \times 29 = \quad 2 \times 696 = 1392$
2 sides at $24 \times 40 = \quad 2 \times 960 = 1920$
2 sides at $29 \times 40 = 2 \times 1160 = 2320$
$$\text{Total} = 5632 \text{ cm}^2$$
This is greater than the net of the cube (5400 cm^2), but as the cube has a slightly smaller volume this is perhaps not surprising. However, a 30.5 cm cube has a larger volume ($28\,373 \text{ cm}^3$) but still has a smaller area (5582 cm^2). A cube is therefore a more economic shape if this type of net is used.

   (d) This type of net is not a practical design because:
   • as there is no overlap, the top and bottom of the box will not be as strong;
   • there will be considerable wastage when the net is cut out of a large sheet of cardboard.

2 (a) Volume = length × width × height
$$= 40 \times 29 \times 24 = 27\,840 \text{ cm}^3$$
   (b) Area = length × width
$$= 128 \times 53$$
$$= 6784 \text{ cm}^2$$

3 (a) The sheet had the following dimensions:
Width = width plus height of box
$$= 24 + 29$$
$$= 53 \text{ cm}$$

Height = twice the sum of the length and width of the box
$$= 2 \times (40 + 24)$$
$$= 2 \times 64$$
$$= 128 \, \text{cm}$$

(b) For boxes of this type, the top and bottom of the box consist of four flaps. Two of these flaps meet in the middle when folded together.

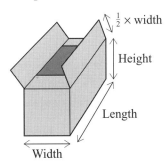

As each of the flaps is half the width of the box, the width of the sheet is the height of the box plus the width of the box (i.e. the two flaps which meet in the middle).

You can also see that when the box is opened out, the length of the resulting sheet needs to make the four sides of the box, so its length must be equal to the length plus width plus length plus width of the box.

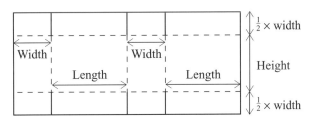

4   The sheet has dimensions width = 60 cm and length = 120 cm.
Area $= 60 \times 120 = 7200 \, \text{cm}^2$

5   (a)   Volume $= 21 \times 37 \times 37 \, \text{cm}^3$
$$= 28\,749 \, \text{cm}^3$$

Note that this is slightly larger than the volume of the actual crisp box.

(b)

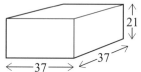

The area of card needed
to make this box is:

$$58 \times 116 = 6728\,\text{cm}^2$$

All dimensions are in cm

(c) This is an improvement on $6890\,\text{cm}^2$, the area of cardboard needed
for the original crisp box. This is therefore a better design as it uses
slightly less cardboard for a slightly greater volume. Grandad was
right.

6 (a) Volume $= 37 \times 37 \times 21$
$\qquad = 28\,749\,\text{cm}^3$

(b) Area $= 148 \times 58 = 8584\,\text{cm}^2$

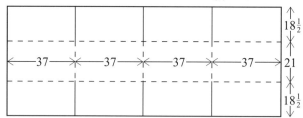

(c) This is not a better design as it uses more cardboard since there is a
greater overlap on the flaps. Because of this, however, it would be
stronger so this design might be preferred if strength was important.

5 Australia

1 and 4(b)

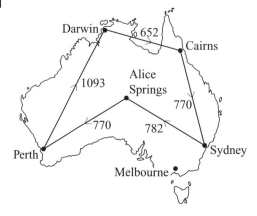

2 (a) Of the cities and towns she was to visit, Perth and Sydney have a minimum temperature of 9°C or approximately 50°F, and Darwin has a maximum temperature of 31°C or approximately 90°F. She used the conversion scale to change from Celsius (°C) to Fahrenheit (°F). (Note that she did not plan to visit Melbourne.)

(b)

	Temperature in August (°F)	
	Maximum	Minimum
Alice Springs	79	50
Cairns	79	63
Darwin	88	70
Melbourne	59	45
Perth	64	48
Sydney	64	48

Clare's range was 50 → 90°F; using the formula you get 48 → 88°F. The formula gives more accurate values.

3 (a) (i) 1760 km   (ii) 1240 km
  (b) 1760 + 1050 + 1240 + 1260 + 1240 = 6550 km

4 (a) 1760 km = 1000 + 700 + 60 km
  $$= 621 + 435 + 37 \text{ miles}$$
  $$= 1093 \text{ miles}$$
  (b) See the diagram in question 1.
  (c) 1093 + 652 + 770 + 782 + 770 = 4067 miles
    or 6·55 × 621 = 4068 miles. (The small difference is due to rounding errors.) 4200 is an over-estimate.

5 (a) £500
  (b) Pounds → ×2·13 → Dollars

    Pounds ← ÷2·13 ← Dollars   and 1 ÷ 2·13 = 0·4694…
                                                 = 47p (to the nearest
                                                         penny)
    To convert pounds to dollars you multiply by 2·13. To convert dollars to pounds you reverse the process and divide by 2·13. This is equivalent to multiplying by 0·47, giving you a conversion rate of 0·47 pounds to the dollar.
  (c) 260 ÷ 2·13 = £122·07   or   260 × 0·47 = £122·20
    (The result is slightly different using the second method because of rounding 0·4694… to 0·47.)

   (d) The local cost of internal flights (in pounds) was:

$$£122·07 + £93·90 + £58·69 + £83·57 + £101·41 = £459·64$$

Clare would save £40·36 if she asked her sister to book all the internal flights. (Even greater savings could be made if Clare bought two coupons in this country and asked her sister to book just three flights!) **Or** you may have answered this question by adding up the cost of all the internal flights in Australian dollars and *then* converting the total into pounds. This gives $979 = £459·62$.

6   $897 × 2·13 = \$1910·61$

6 The painter's problem

1 (a) $\frac{1}{2}$

If he mixed paint in the ratio 1 : 1, then 2 litres of the mixture would contain 1 litre of red and 1 litre of blue. The fraction of the mixture which was red was therefore '1 out of 2', i.e. $\frac{1}{2}$.

  (b) $\frac{2}{3}$

If he mixed paint in the ratio 1 : 2, then 3 litres of the mixture would contain 1 litre of red and 2 litres of blue. The fraction of the mixture which was blue was therefore '2 out of 3', i.e. $\frac{2}{3}$.

  (c) In a 2 : 5 mixture, if you mix 2 litres of red paint with 5 litres of blue you will get 7 litres of the mixture. 2 out of the 7 litres are therefore red paint so the fraction is $\frac{2}{7}$.

2   He would need $2\frac{1}{2}$ litres of blue paint. A 2 :5 mix is the same as a 1 : $2\frac{1}{2}$ mix. The ratios are the same.

3   In the correct mixture, 28·6% of the mixture was red ($\frac{2}{7} = 0·2857... = 28·6\%$). With a 3 : 7 mix 30% of the mixture would be red. ($\frac{3}{10} = 0·3 = 30\%$.) There would therefore be too much red in such a mixture.

4   $5\,m + 3\,m + 1·5\,m + 2\,m + 3·5\,m + 5\,m = 20\,m$

5   If you imagine the room 'opened out' it would look like a rectangle 20 m long and 2·5 m high.

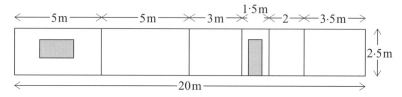

Area = length × height
        = 20 × 2·5
        = 50 m²

6   There were 50 m² of wall needing two coats of paint so he needed enough paint for 100 m². One litre of paint covers 12 m² so he needed 100 ÷ 12 = 8·33 litres.

7   There are two ways he may have calculated this:
    (i)   He could have calculated $\frac{5}{7}$ of 8·33 litres:

$$\frac{1}{7} \text{ of } 8\cdot33 \text{ litres} = 8\cdot33 \div 7$$
$$= 1\cdot19 \text{ litres}$$
$$\frac{5}{7} \text{ of } 8\cdot33 \text{ litres} = 1\cdot19 \times 5$$
$$= 5\cdot95 \text{ litres}$$

    (ii) He could have subtracted the 2·38 litres of paint from the 8·33 litres of mixture:
          8·33 − 2·38 = 5·95 litres

7 Landscaping

1   This way he would never under-estimate quantities. It would be inconvenient to have to order a few extra turfs and to have to return at a later date to complete the job. It would be better to throw some away if they were not needed.

2   He used a ruler calibrated in centimetres and millimetres. He measured lengths to the nearest millimetre when constructing the drawing. (The height of his triangle was in fact 15·8 cm which represented a distance of 15·8 yd on the ground, but he rounded this up to 16 yd to ensure that he over-estimated the area.)

3

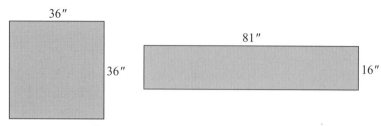

$36 \times 36 = 1296$ in^2 $81 \times 16 = 1296$ in^2

4   (a) Area $= \frac{1}{2} \times$ base $\times$ height   Area $= \frac{1}{2} \times$ base $\times$ height
               $= \frac{1}{2} \times 36 \times 16$ $= \frac{1}{2} \times 25 \times 26$
               $= 288$ yd^2 $= 325$ yd^2

    (b) The total area in square yards is $288 + 325 = 613$ yd^2.

5   The wild flower area was approximately a 9 m by 16 m rectangle.
    The area was therefore $9 \times 16 = 144$ m^2.
    The supplier recommended 50 grams of seed per square metre.
    He would need $144 \times 50 = 7200$ grams
                            $= 7 \cdot 2$ kg
    $2 \times 2 \cdot 5 = 5$ kg   so 2 bags would not be enough.
    $3 \times 2 \cdot 5 = 7 \cdot 5$ kg   so 3 bags would be more than enough (just).

6   $651 \div 620 = 1 \cdot 05$ so the cost was £1·05 per turf.
    $45 \div 3 = 15$ so the cost was £15 per bag.

7   Check: $1000 + 651 + 45 = £1696$
    Check: $1696 \times 0 \cdot 175 = £296 \cdot 80$ (note that $17 \cdot 5\% = 0 \cdot 175$)
    Check: $1696 + 296 \cdot 80 = £1992 \cdot 80$

8 House prices

1   (a) £460 000 – £24 000 = £436 000
    (b) £105 000 – £34 000 = £71 000
    (c) There seemed to be less variation of house prices in Portly, which may
         indicate less variation in the housing stock (type of housing available).

2   (a) £675 000
    (b) £1 056 000

3   (a) Mean
    (b) £675 000 ÷ 9 = £75 000,   £1 056 000 ÷ 12 = £88 000

4 (a) The mean selling price was substantially higher for Ashfield (by £13 000),
       implying more expensive housing and hence more affluent owners!
       Although the mean was higher, most of the housing was quite modest
       compared with the number of detached houses in Portly. The figure
       was greatly influenced by just two properties (and one in particular),
       and so it is questionable whether the mean was in fact an accurate
       representation of the 'average' housing in Ashfield.

   (b) Another approach is to compare 'like with like'. For example,
       3-bedroomed detached houses appeared to sell for higher prices in Portly
       than in Ashfield, suggesting that Portly was the more affluent area.

   (c) **Portly** £ 34 000   **Ashfield** £ 24 000
               £ 45 000   £ 24 000   Mode
               £ 68 000   £ 28 000   £24 000
               £ 75 000   £ 31 000
               £ 82 000←Median £82 000   £ 38 000
               £ 84 000   No mode exists.   £ 44 000 ← Median
               £ 87 000   £ 48 000   £46 000
               £ 95 000   £ 50 000
               £105 000   £ 65 000
                                                          £ 70 000
                                                          £105 000
                                                          £460 000

   (d) The median
       No modal value exists for Portly and the mode for Ashfield of £24 000
       obviously does not give an accurate representation of its housing stock.
       The median has the advantage of not letting very small or large values
       have too great an impact. In this case the median is preferable to the
       mean as a representative value for comparison although, as indicated in
       (b) above, comparing 'like with like' is probably a more sensible approach.

5 (a) Three similar houses, 3-bedroomed detached, in the Portly district
       sold for £82 000, £84 000 and £87 000 – hence £80 000 to £90 000
       would seem a sensible range to quote.

   (b) Two 3-bedroomed detached houses were sold in Ashfield for £65 000
       and £70 000. Although this is very limited information, any valuation
       was likely to be well below that for a similar house in Portly. It may
       have been anywhere in the range £60 000 to £75 000.

6 He used past evidence of sales to predict the probability of selling a house
   within a given period. He had only sold one out of the ten houses, within
   the required period, for more than £85 000.
   1 out of 10 is equivalent to $\frac{1}{10}$ or 10%.

7 Winston sold five of the ten houses (50%) for £80 000 or more; four in the £80 000 to £85 000 range and one for more than £85 000. This figure was only a rough guide to what may happen in the future, but it would seem the client did have a fair chance of selling her house if she was prepared to accept an offer in the region of £82 000. If she were to accept an offer substantially below this £82 000, she could have optimistically expected her chance of selling the property to improve beyond 50%.

9 Relative business

1 Marita's monthly expenses averaged £1050 + £560 = £1610.
Over the year this amounted to 12 × £1610 = £19 320.
£42 750 − £19 320 = £23 430
Dara's profit was similarly calculated: monthly expenses and rent came to £1255, so annual expenses and rent were 12 × £1255 = £15 060.
£35 210 − £15 060 = £20 150

2 Mean profit = total profit ÷ number of years, i.e. £101 250 ÷ 5 = £20 250
Range = highest profit − lowest profit, i.e. £23 430 − £17 110 = £6320

3 Using the same methods,
Dara's total profit in £ was $^{-}$5110 + $^{-}$3330 + 760 + 9580 + 20 150 = 22 050.
So her mean profit was £22 050 ÷ 5 = £4410.
Her range was £20 150 − ($^{-}$£5110) = £20 150 + £5110 = £25 260.

4 The ranges were very different because:
 • Marita took over a going concern whilst Dara built up trade from scratch;
 • Marita did not have the large initial expenses of Dara.

5 (a) Using minus signs   (b) by points below the horizontal axis.

6

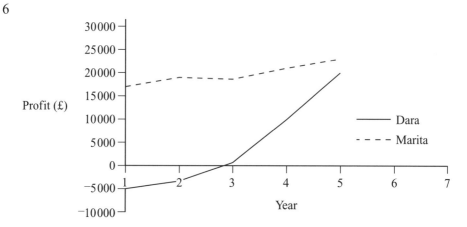

7 (a) By extending the graph you might predict that with sustained growth, Marita's profits would be about £25 000 in year 6 and about £27 000 in year 7. Dara's rate of growth seems more dramatic and if you think she could maintain this, then you might predict profits of about £33 000 in year 6 and about £49 000 in year 7.

   (b) Using these figures:
   • Dara's total profit over 7 years would be about £104 000.
     Mean = 104 000 ÷ 7 = £14 857
   • Marita's total profit over 7 years would be about £153 000.
     Mean = 153 000 ÷ 7 = £21 857

   It is very unlikely that Dara's mean profit over the seven years would be greater than Marita's.

10 Cycle computer

1 You should find the same number, 208, in each case.

2 (a) $15 \div 1\cdot61 = 9\cdot3$ m.p.h.
   (b) Because 1 mile = 1·61 km, the number of miles in a given distance is *fewer* than the number of kilometres, in the ratio 1·61:1.

3 (a) Circumference = $386 \times 3\cdot14 = 1212$ mm
   (b) Input number for km = $1212 \div 10 = 121$ (to nearest whole number)
   (c) Input number for miles = $121 \div 1\cdot61 = 75$ (to nearest whole number)

4 The multiplier is $25\cdot4 \div 1\cdot61 \div 10$ (missing out stage B of A–E, which converted from diameter to circumference). The required number is 1·58.

5 (a) $2089 \div 16\cdot1 = 129\cdot75 \approx 130$. This shows that '$\div 1\cdot61 \div 10$' is the same as '$\div (1\cdot61 \times 10)$'.
   (b) $n = 2110 \div 16\cdot1 = 131$ (to nearest whole number)

6 (a) A   Wheel diameter = 24·8 inches
       B $24\cdot8 \times 3\cdot14 = 77\cdot87$
       C $77\cdot87 \times 25\cdot4 = 1978$
       D $1978 \div 1\cdot61 = 1229$
       E $1229 \div 10 = 123$ (to nearest whole number)
       $n = 123$
   (b) A   Wheel diameter = 24·8 inches
       B $24\cdot8 \times 4\cdot95 = 123$ (to nearest whole number)
       $n = 123$
   (c) $3\cdot14 \times 25\cdot4 \div 1\cdot61 \div 10 = 4\cdot95$ (to 2 decimal places). The string of operations in B – E can be replaced by a single multiplication.

11 Planning permission

1. (a) Base area of cylinder $= \pi r^2$
$$= \pi \times 5\cdot1 \times 5\cdot1$$
$$= 81\cdot7128\ldots \text{ m}^2$$
Volume of cylinder $=$ base area $\times$ height
$$= 81\cdot7128\ldots \times 5\cdot4$$
$$= 441\cdot25 \text{ m}^3$$

   (b) Volume $=$ base area $\times$ height $\div 3$
$$= 81\cdot7128\ldots \times 2\cdot2 \div 3$$
$$= 59\cdot92 \text{ m}^3$$

   (c) $441\cdot25 + 59\cdot92 = 501\cdot17 \text{ m}^3$

   (d) $6 \times 4\cdot5 \times 2\cdot4 = 64\cdot8 \text{ m}^3$

   (e) Volume $=$ area of triangle $\times$ length of prism
$$= (\tfrac{1}{2} \times 4\cdot5 \times 1\cdot0) \times 6$$
$$= 13\cdot5 \text{ m}^3$$

   (f) $64\cdot8 + 13\cdot5 = 78\cdot3 \text{ m}^3$

2. Volume must not exceed 15% of the volume of the house.
15% of $501\cdot17 \text{ m}^3 = 0\cdot15 \times 501\cdot17$
$$= 75\cdot18 \text{ m}^3$$

3. The volume of the extension would be:

$$(4\cdot5 \times 5\cdot76 \times 2\cdot4) + (\tfrac{1}{2} \times 4\cdot5 \times 1\cdot0 \times 5\cdot76) = 75\cdot17 \text{ m}^3$$

   If the length was reduced to $5\cdot77$ m then the volume would be $75\cdot30 \text{ m}^3$ which would be above the limit, so she is correct in her calculation.

4.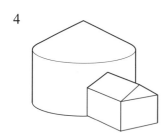

Core skill techniques

1 Number

1.1 Fractions, decimals, percentages and ratios

1.1.1 Fractions

A fraction has two parts, a **numerator** and a **denominator**.

$$\text{Fraction} = \frac{\text{numerator}}{\text{denominator}}$$

In the fraction 'three-eights', the numerator is 3 and the denominator is 8.

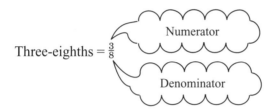

Three-eighths $= \frac{3}{8}$

Any fraction has many equivalent forms.

Example 1

Write down at least five fractions equivalent to $\frac{1}{2}$.

Solution

$\frac{1}{2} = \frac{2}{4} = \frac{3}{6} = \frac{4}{8} = \frac{5}{10} = \ldots$ and so on.

Given any fraction, you can write down an equivalent fraction by simply multiplying the numerator and denominator by the same number.

For example, $\frac{3}{5}$ and $\frac{21}{35}$ are equivalent fractions.

---

1   Which of these fractions are equivalent to three-eights?

(a) $\frac{6}{16}$ (b) $\frac{9}{24}$ (c) $\frac{15}{40}$ (d) $\frac{10}{25}$ (e) $\frac{30}{80}$ (f) $\frac{240}{640}$

Solution – page 96

To add or subtract two fractions, you must first use the idea of equivalent fractions to write both fractions so that they have the same denominator. You can find a common denominator by multiplying together the denominators of the two fractions.

Example 2

Calculate $\frac{3}{4} - \frac{2}{5}$.

Solution

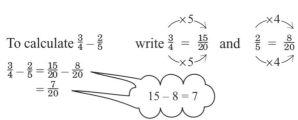

To calculate $\frac{3}{4} - \frac{2}{5}$ write $\frac{3}{4} = \frac{15}{20}$ and $\frac{2}{5} = \frac{8}{20}$

$\frac{3}{4} - \frac{2}{5} = \frac{15}{20} - \frac{8}{20}$
$= \frac{7}{20}$

$15 - 8 = 7$

Once you have written the fractions as the same type of fraction (i.e. they have the same denominator), you can add or subtract them by simply adding or subtracting the numerators (*not* the denominators).

You can show equivalence using a diagram where the shaded part of a square represents the fraction.

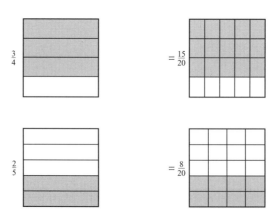

2 Calculate: (a) $\frac{3}{4} + \frac{2}{5}$ (b) $\frac{2}{3} + \frac{4}{5}$ (c) $\frac{5}{8} - \frac{1}{3}$

Solution – page 96

1.1.2 Decimals

It is easy to write a fraction as a decimal if you use a calculator.

Example 3

Write $\frac{3}{8}$ as a decimal.

Solution

$\frac{3}{8}$ means '3 divided by 8'.

You can divide 3 by 8 using a calculator.

$\frac{3}{8} = 3 \div 8 = 0 \cdot 375$

---

3 Write these fractions as decimals:

(a) $\frac{1}{2}$ (b) $\frac{3}{4}$ (c) $\frac{5}{8}$ (d) $\frac{7}{16}$ (e) $\frac{35}{100}$ (f) $\frac{3}{7}$

Solution – page 96

Some decimals carry on for ever and it is necessary to round them to a number of decimal places.

Example 4

Round the decimal $0 \cdot 428\,571\,42\ldots$ to:

(a) 1 decimal place,

(b) 2 decimal places,

(c) 3 decimal places.

Solution

$\downarrow$

(a) $0 \cdot 428\,571\,42\ldots = 0 \cdot 4$ (to 1 d.p.)

The 4 is not rounded up because the next digit, 2, is less than 5 and so the decimal is nearer $0 \cdot 4$ than $0 \cdot 5$.

$\downarrow$

(b) $0 \cdot 428\,571\,42\ldots = 0 \cdot 43$ (to 2 d.p.)

The 2 *is* rounded up to 3 because the next digit, 8, *is not* less than 5 and so the decimal is nearer $0 \cdot 43$ than $0 \cdot 42$.

$\downarrow$

(c) $0 \cdot 428\,571\,42\ldots = 0 \cdot 429$ (to 3 d.p.)

The 8 is rounded up to 9 because the next digit, 5, is not less than 5 and so the decimal is nearer $0 \cdot 429$ than $0 \cdot 428$.

---

4 Round each of these decimals to: (i) 1 decimal place,
                                        (ii) 2 decimal places,
                                        (iii) 3 decimal places.

(a) $0 \cdot 384\,326$ (b) $0 \cdot 545\,621$ (c) $0 \cdot 296\,321\,9$

Solution – page 96

1.1.3 Percentages

A **percentage**, %, is a special type of fraction; it is a fraction of one hundred. The two noughts in the percentage sign remind you that the fraction is out of a hundred and the '/' reminds you that it is a fraction.

Example 5

Express 45% as a decimal.

Solution

$$45\% = \frac{45}{100}$$

$$= 45 \div 100$$

$$= 0 \cdot 45$$

% means $\frac{1}{100}$

Example 6

Express 45% as a fraction in its simplest form.

Solution

$$45\% = \frac{45}{100} = \frac{9}{20}$$

$$\frac{45}{100} \overset{\div 5}{\underset{\div 5}{=}} \frac{9}{20}$$

So $45\% = \frac{9}{20}$

To calculate a percentage of a quantity, it is easiest to write the percentage as a decimal and then use a calculator to multiply by the decimal.

Example 7

Find 15% of £36.

Solution

$$15\% = 0 \cdot 15$$

$$15\% \text{ of } £36 = 0 \cdot 15 \times 36$$

$$= 5 \cdot 4$$

$$= £5 \cdot 40$$

---

5 Work out:

(a) a 25% discount on a mobile phone costing £37·60,

(b) the VAT (at 17·5%) on a pair of shoes costing £19·99.

Solution – page 97

To express a fraction as a percentage, use a calculator to express the fraction as a decimal, then write the decimal as a percentage.

Example 8

Write $\frac{244}{360}$ as a percentage.

Solution

$$244 \div 360 = 0 \cdot 677\,777\,77\ldots$$
$$= 0 \cdot 68 \quad \text{(rounded to two decimal places)}$$
$$= 68\% \quad \text{(or } 67 \cdot 8\% \text{ if a more accurate value is required)}$$

---

6   Write these fractions as percentages:

(a) $\frac{1}{2}$ (b) $\frac{3}{4}$ (c) $\frac{5}{8}$ (d) $\frac{7}{16}$ (e) $\frac{3}{7}$ (f) $\frac{135}{600}$

Solution – page 97

1.1.4 Ratios

If you mix yellow and blue paint you get green paint. The shade of green depends on the **ratio** of yellow to blue. If you mix 2 tins of yellow with 3 tins of blue then the ratio of yellow to blue is two to three. The mathematical shorthand for this is $2 : 3$.

Example 9

If you mix yellow and blue paint in the ratio $2 : 3$, what fraction of the mixture is yellow?

Solution

If you mix, say, 2 litres of yellow with 3 litres of blue you get 5 litres of the mixture. The fraction of this mixture which is yellow is $\frac{2}{5}$. (Note that $\frac{3}{5}$ of the mixture will be blue.)

Example 10

Two workers, Alan and Beth, are paid £120 between them for a job of work. Alan works 3 hours on the job and Beth works 5 hours, so the money is divided between them in the ratio $3 : 5$. (Read $3 : 5$ as 'three to five'.) How much does Alan receive?

Solution

Between them they worked 8 hours. Alan worked 3 of these hours so his share was $\frac{3}{8}$ of the £120. (Beth worked 5 hours so her share was $\frac{5}{8}$ of £120.)

To calculate Alan's share, first work out $\frac{1}{8}$ of £120:

$$\frac{1}{8} \times 120 = 120 \div 8$$
$$= £15$$

$$\frac{3}{8} \times 120 = 3 \times 15$$
$$= £45$$

so Alan's share was £45. (Beth received £75.)

---

7 Explain why the money would have been divided up the same if Alan had worked 6 hours and Beth had worked 10 hours at the job.

Solution – page 97

The ratio $3:4$ is the same as $6:8$. In fact the ratio $3:4$ can be written in many equivalent ways (just as a fraction has many equivalent fractions).

$$
\begin{array}{ccc}
3:4 & 3:4 & 3:4 \\
\times 2 \Big\downarrow\Big\downarrow \times 2 & \times 5 \Big\downarrow\Big\downarrow \times 5 & \times 10 \Big\downarrow\Big\downarrow \times 10 \\
6:8 & 15:20 & 30:40
\end{array}
$$

---

8 (a) Show that the ratio $3:5$ is equivalent to $45:75$.
   (b) Explain the connection between the ratio $45:75$ and the solution to example 10.
   (c) Alan and Beth are paid £360 for another job. Alan works 15 hours while Beth only works 10 hours. Calculate Alan's share of the money.

Solution – page 97

Further practice and applications: *Tin can labels (page 6)*
The painter's problem (page 21)
Landscaping (page 24)
Cycle computer (page 32)
Planning permission (page 35)

1.2 Probability descriptions

The chance (likelihood) of some event happening can be any value from zero probability (no chance) to a probability of one (certain to happen).

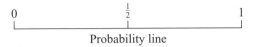

Probability line

Probabilities are fractions and can be represented by decimal fractions, ordinary fractions or percentage fractions. They are useful for giving an indication of how likely you think a prediction is.

Example 1

Leena works in a factory which manufactures fireworks. It is inevitable that some of the fireworks produced will fail to explode. Obviously it is not sensible to test all the fireworks produced! She takes a sample of 20 fireworks and tests them. Only 17 explode. What is the probability that any firework taken from the production line will fail to explode?

Solution

If 17 exploded, then 3 must have failed to explode. That is, 3 out of 20 failed.

On this evidence it is reasonable to predict that the probability of any one firework failing is $\frac{3}{20}$.

1 (a) Write the probability $\frac{3}{20}$:
      (i) as a decimal,   (ii) as a percentage.
   (b) Leena (example 1) takes another sample from a different production line, but this time she tests only 15 fireworks. Of these 15, again 3 fail to explode. Use this second example to estimate the probability that a firework from the second production line will fail. Write your answer as:
      (i) a fraction,   (ii) a decimal,   (iii) a percentage.
   (c) Copy the probability line shown above and mark with an arrow the probability that a firework will fail when selected from:
      (i) the first production line,   (ii) the second production line.
   (d) On this evidence, which production line is more reliable?

Solution – page 97

Further practice and applications: *House prices (page 27)*

1.3 Negative numbers

Negative numbers are used to denote values below zero. (Numbers which are greater than zero are called **positive numbers**.)

Positive and negative numbers can, for example, be used to represent profit and loss. In this context, a loss is a 'negative profit'.

Suppose you rent a stall at a craft fair at a cost of £10 per day.
- If you make £16 on the goods you sell, then you make a profit of £6 because $16 - 10 = 6$.
- If you make £10 on the goods you sell, you break even (i.e. you make zero profit) because $10 - 10 = 0$.
- If you make just £6 on the goods you sell, you make a loss of £4. Your profit is negative because $6 - 10 = {}^-4$.

> Note that negative numbers are shown with a 'negative' sign. Positive numbers have no sign.

Example 1

Sue rents a stall at a craft fair for £10 a day. Her profits on 5 days are:

Day	1	2	3	4	5
Profit (£)	6	0	$^-4$	$^-1$	12

What is her total profit over the five days?

Solution

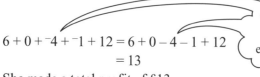

> To add a negative number you simply *subtract* the equivalent positive number.

$$6 + 0 + {}^-4 + {}^-1 + 12 = 6 + 0 - 4 - 1 + 12$$
$$= 13$$

She made a total profit of £13.

---

1 Work out:

(a) $4 + {}^-2$ (b) $15 + {}^-6$ (c) ${}^-5 + {}^-3$

(d) $5 + {}^-5$ (e) $5 + {}^-8$ (f) $5 + {}^-33$

Solution – page 98

Example 2

In summer the maximum temperature is 38°C and the minimum temperature is 12°C. In winter the maximum is 14°C and the minimum is $^-7$°C.

What is the range in: (a) the summer,
                        (b) the winter?

Solution

Range = maximum temperature − minimum temperature

(a)   38 − 12 = 26°C

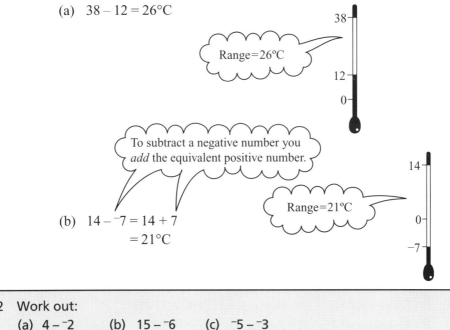

(b)   14 − ⁻7 = 14 + 7
          = 21°C

---

2   Work out:
   (a) 4 − ⁻2   (b) 15 − ⁻6   (c) ⁻5 − ⁻3
   (d) ⁻5 − ⁻5   (e) ⁻5 − ⁻8   (f) 5 − ⁻33

Solution – page 98

Further practice and applications: *Relative business (page 29)*

1.4 Estimation, prediction and checking procedures

Although it is sensible to use a calculator to carry out calculations to ensure accuracy, errors do occasionally occur because the calculator has not been used correctly. It is important to be aware of what checking procedures can be carried out to try to prevent this happening.

You can:
• repeat a calculation and see if you still get the same answer;
• carry out the calculation in a different way;
• work backwards from the answer;
• estimate what the answer should be approximately.

Example 1

You sell a number of items and calculate the total:

£123·50 + £43 + £78·99 + £2·66 = £248·15

How could you carry out this calculation in a different way?

Solution

People often check their addition by adding the numbers in reverse order:

£2·66 + £78·99 + £43 + £123·50 = £248·15

Example 2

You sell something for £260 less 15% discount. You calculate the final selling price to be:

Cost	£260
Less 15%	£ 39 —
Total	£221

$0·15 \times 260 = 39$

How could you carry out this calculation in a different way?

Solution

You know that if you deduct 15% then you have 85% left, so you can check the final answer by calculating 85% of £260. You should get £221.

---

1   (a) In example 2, check that 85% of £260 is £221.

   (b) In example 1, check that £2·66 + £78·99 + £43 + £123·50 gives the correct total.

Solution – page 98

Example 3

Three children share 45 sweets equally between them.
They each get 45 ÷ 3 = 15 sweets.
How could you work backwards from the answer to check this?

Solution

You *divide by 3* to get an answer, so if you start with the answer and *multiply by 3*, you get back to where you started.

i.e., if 45 ÷ **3** = 15 then 15 × **3** = 45

---

2   Seven workers share £244 equally. They each get:

£244 ÷ 7 = £34·86

$244 ÷ 7 = 34·857\ 142...$
$= 34·86$ (rounded to 2 d.p.)

Check this division by multiplication.

Solution – page 98

Example 4

John buys 4·8 metres of material at £23·50 a metre. Show how you can estimate the cost.

Solution

Round 4·8 m up to 5 m and round £23·50 down to £20.
The cost is about $5 \times £20 = £100$.
In fact, the cost is $4·8 \times £23·50 = £112·80$.

Rounding figures so that you can do a quick calculation *in your head* is a useful skill. The result, although not accurate, gives an indication of what to expect. It is an **estimation**.

> 3 Round the following numbers and estimate the answer by doing a quick calculation in your head:
> (a) 279×213 (b) $392 \div 48$ (c) $5·78 \times 18·87$
>
> **Solution – page 98**

Whether or not you do an approximate calculation, you should *always* look at the result of a calculation and check if it is reasonable. Is it the sort of figure you might have *predicted*?

Example 5

It takes a secretary 30 minutes to type 1300 words.
She calculates that she does $30 \div 1300$ words per minute.
Is the answer she gets reasonable?

Solution

Before she carries out the calculation she might think to herself that a typist can be expected to type 50 to 60 words per minute. The calculation gives:

$$30 \div 1300 = 0·023\,07\ldots$$

This is clearly so different from what she predicted that she knows something has gone wrong. She might have entered the calculation into her calculator incorrectly so the first thing she does is check the calculation. In this case the calculation is correct. The problem here is that it is the wrong calculation for solving this problem.

4 (a) What is the correct calculation for solving the problem in example 5?
(b) Calculate how many words per minute the secretary types.

Solution – page 99

Further practice and applications: *Tin can labels (page 6)*
Australia (page 18)
Relative business (page 29)

1.5 Formulas in words and symbols

Formulas are sometimes expressed in words.

Example 1

Write down a formula for the distance a vehicle travels in a given time when travelling at a given speed.

Solution

Distance = speed × time

To use a formula such as this you simply substitute the words in the formula with the appropriate numbers.

Example 2

Work out how far a car travels in 3 hours if its average speed is 45 miles per hour (m.p.h.).

Solution

Speed = 45 and time = 3

So distance = speed × time
$$= 45 \times 3$$
$$= 135 \text{ miles}$$

Don't forget the *units* in your final answer.

It is common practice in mathematics to replace a word with a symbol (usually a letter). In the formula used in the example, you might replace the word *distance* with the letter d, the word *speed* with the letter s and the word *time* with the letter t. In this case the formula becomes:

$$d = s \times t$$

This is an **algebraic** formula. In algebra letters are used to represent numbers. It is also common to leave out the multiplication sign in algebra, so the formula could be written:

$$d = st$$

Example 3

Use the algebraic formula $a = 2b + c$ to find a when $b = 5$ and $c = 7$.

Solution

$$a = 2b + c$$
$$= 2 \times b + c$$
$$= 2 \times 5 + 7$$
$$= 10 + 7$$
$$= 17$$

> *2b* means '2 multipled by *b*.'

> Always do the multiplication before the addition.

---

1 Use the formula $p = 3q - 5r$ to calculate the value of p when $q = 9$ and $r = 4$.

Solution – page 99

If you square a number, then you multiply it by itself. Squares are sometimes used in formulas.

Example 4

Find c where $c = 3r^2$ and $r = 5$.

Solution

$$c = 3 \times 5^2$$
$$= 3 \times 5 \times 5$$
$$= 75$$

> Note that 5^2 is just a shorthand way of writing 5×5.

---

2 Use the formula $p = 3q^2 - 5r$ to calculate the value of p when $q = 6$ and $r = 4$.

Solution – page 99

Further practice and applications: *Crisp boxes (page 15)*
Australia (page 18)
Cycle computer (page 32)
Planning permission (page 35)

2 Shape, space and measure

2.1 Units of measurement

The basic measurements in shape and space are **length**, **mass** ('weight')
and **time**.

The units of time are:

There are just over 52 weeks in a year.

60 seconds = 1 minute
60 minutes = 1 hour
24 hours = 1 day
7 days = 1 week

There are 365 days in a year, except
in a leap year when there are 366.

The units of mass are:

Metric measures	**Imperial measures**
1000 grams (g) = 1 kilogram (kg)	16 ounces (oz) = 1 pound (lb)
1000 kilograms = 1 tonne	14 pounds = 1 stone (st)
	2240 pounds = 1 ton

Metric measures are used as a standard in most industries. However, there are
some job situations where the old British imperial measurements are still used.
You sometimes have to convert between the two and it is useful to know that:
• 1 kilogram is approximately 2·2 pounds;
• 1 ton is approximately 1 tonne.
Some job situations may require more accurate conversions.

The units of length are:

Metric measures	**Imperial measures**
10 millimetres (mm) = 1 centimetre (cm)	12 inches (" or in) = 1 foot (' or ft)
100 centimetres = 1 metre (m)	3 feet = 1 yard
1000 millimetres = 1 metre	1760 yards = 1 mile
1000 metres = 1 kilometre (km)	220 yards = 1 furlong
	8 furlongs = 1 mile

It is useful to know that:
• 1 foot is approximately 30 cm;
• 1 inch is approximately 2·5 cm;
• 1 mile is approximately 1600 m.

The units of area and volume are based on those of length. For example, you might measure the area of a carpet in square metres (m^2) or square yards (yd^2). Similarly, you might measure the volume of earth dug out of a foundation in cubic metres (m^3). However, volumes also have their own units, particularly where the volume refers to a fluid. You might buy a pint of beer or a litre of orange juice. These are units of capacity.

The units of capacity are:

Metric measures	**Imperial measures**
1000 millilitres (ml) = 1 litre (l)	20 fluid ounces = 1 pint
100 centilitres (cl) = 1 litre	8 pints = 1 gallon
1000 litres = 1 cubic metre (m^3)	

It is useful to know that:
• 1 litre is approximately 0·22 gallons;
• there are roughly 2 pints to a litre;
• 1 millilitre is precisely the same as 1 cubic centimetre.

---

1 (a) Samantha weighs 8 stone 5 pounds (8 st 5 lb).
        (i) What does she weigh in pounds?
        (ii) What is her approximate weight in kilograms?
    (b) An oil tank contains 1200 litres. What is this approximately in gallons?
    (c) A room is 8 feet 6 inches high (8'6"). What is this approximately in metres?
    (d) 5 miles is approximately how many kilometres?
    Solution – page 99

Special units of area are used in agriculture and in the building industry for measuring large areas:
• 1 acre = 4840 square yards;
• 1 hectare = 10 000 square metres;
• 1 hectare is approximately 2·5 acres.

Further practice and applications: *Landscaping (page 24)*

2.2 2-dimensional problems – perimeter and area

2.2.1 Rectangular shapes

A plane shape is a shape drawn on a flat surface. The area of the shape is measured by the number of squares enclosed by the shape.

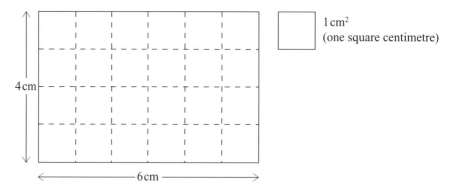

1 cm² (one square centimetre)

24 little squares fit in the large rectangle. The rectangle has area $6 \times 4 = 24\ \text{cm}^2$.

You can always calculate the area of a rectangle using the formula:

$$\text{area} = \text{base} \times \text{height}$$

even when there is not a whole number of squares.

Example 1
   Calculate the area of this rectangle.

Solution

   Area = base × height
      $= 5\cdot4 \times 2\cdot6$
      $= 14\cdot04\ \text{cm}^2$

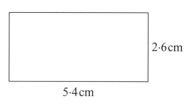

2·6 cm

5·4 cm

The **perimeter** of a shape is the distance around the outside of the shape. The perimeter of the rectangle in example 1 is $(5\cdot4 + 2\cdot6 + 5\cdot4 + 2\cdot6)\ \text{cm} = 16\cdot0\ \text{cm}$.

1 For the shape shown here, calculate:
 (a) the perimeter,
 (b) the area.
  (Hint: think of the shape as being two
  rectangles stuck together.)

Solution – page 100

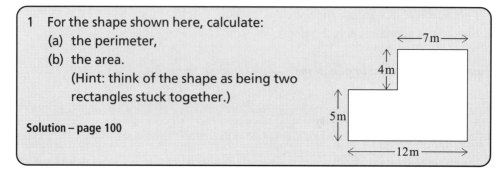

2.2.2 Triangles

A triangle is half a rectangle.

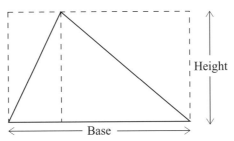

You calculate the area of a triangle using the formula:

$$\text{area} = \tfrac{1}{2}(\text{base} \times \text{height})$$

Example 2

Calculate the area of this triangle.

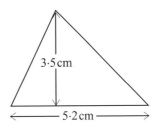

Solution

$$\begin{aligned}
\text{Area} &= \tfrac{1}{2}(\text{base} \times \text{height}) \\
&= \tfrac{1}{2}(5{\cdot}2 \times 3{\cdot}5) \\
&= \tfrac{1}{2} \times 18{\cdot}2 \\
&= 9{\cdot}1\ \text{cm}^2
\end{aligned}$$

---

2 **Calculate the area of this triangle.**

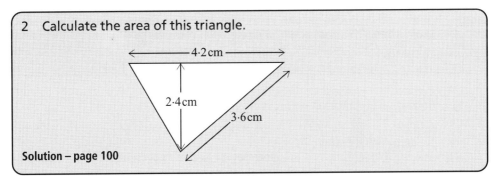

Solution – page 100

2.2.3 Circles

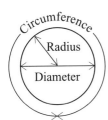

Circumference is the name given to the distance around the outside (i.e. the perimeter) of a circle.

The circumference is roughly three times the diameter.

If you need to calculate the circumference accurately, use the formula:

$$\text{circumference} = \text{pi} \times \text{diameter}$$
$$c = \pi d$$

The constant π (called pi) is found on your calculator.
Press π and your calculator will show:

$$3.141592654$$

Example 3

Calculate the circumference of a circle with diameter 8 cm.

Solution

Press $\boxed{\pi}$ $\boxed{\times}$ $\boxed{8}$ $\boxed{=}$

$c = \pi \times d$
$\quad = \pi \times 8$
$\quad = 25.1327\ldots$

Circumference is 25.1 cm   (to the nearest mm).

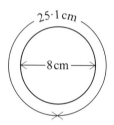

Sometimes you are given the **radius** rather than the diameter of a circle. The radius is the distance from the centre of a circle to the circumference. The radius is half the diameter.

> **3   Calculate the circumference of a circle with radius 3 m.**
>
> **Solution – page 100**

To calculate accurately the area within a circle use the formula:

$$\text{area} = \text{pi} \times \text{radius}^2$$
$$A = \pi r^2$$
$$\quad = \pi \times r \times r$$

Note that the 'square' applies only to the radius

Example 4

Calculate the area of a circle with radius 5.2 cm.

Solution

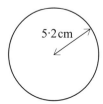

$A = \pi \times 5.2 \times 5.2$
$\quad = 84.948\,665\ldots$

Area is 85 cm^2 (to the nearest square cm).

Example 5

Calculate the area of a circle with diameter 7 m.

Solution

The radius is half the diameter.

$r = 3.5\,\text{m}$
$A = \pi \times 3.5 \times 3.5$
$\quad = 38.484\,510\ldots$
$\quad\quad 38.5\,\text{m}^2$ (to the nearest tenth of
$\quad\quad\quad$ a square metre)

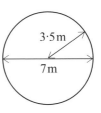

4 Calculate:
   (a) the perimeter,
   (b) the area
   of this semicircle.

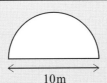

10m

Solution – page 100

Further practice and applications: *Tin can labels (page 6)*
Crisp boxes (page 15)
The painter's problem (page 21)
Landscaping (page 24)
Cycle computer (page 32)

2.3 3-dimensional problems – volumes

The world you live and work in is three-dimensional (3-D). It has length, width and height. The world of information and communication (paper, pictures, computer monitors, TV and so on), is usually two-dimensional (2-D). It has no depth. There are several ways of portraying the 3-D world on a 2-D medium. A photograph or painting does this very effectively.

Many everyday objects are box-shaped (cuboids) and these can easily be drawn using isometric (triangular dotted) paper.

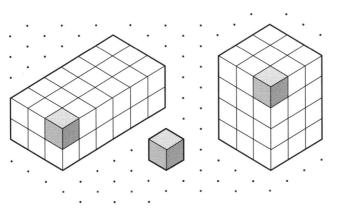

The space contained within an object is its volume. You measure the volume by counting how many small cubes will fit inside the object. The isometric drawing on page 71 shows two cuboids each with a volume of 36 cm³.

The volume of a cuboid is calculated using the formula:

volume = width × height × depth

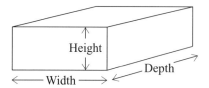

If the unit for length is a centimetre then the unit for volume is cm³ (cubic centimetres); if the unit of length is a metre then the unit for volume is m³ (cubic metres). The symbol '3' is used because you multiply a length by a length by a length to calculate volume.

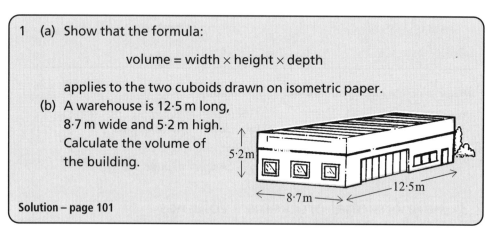

1   (a) Show that the formula:

volume = width × height × depth

applies to the two cuboids drawn on isometric paper.
(b) A warehouse is 12·5 m long, 8·7 m wide and 5·2 m high. Calculate the volume of the building.

5·2 m
8·7 m
12·5 m

Solution – page 101

A box made out of cardboard starts life as a two-dimensional sheet of card. Any 3-D cuboid can be 'opened up' to give its 2-D **net**.

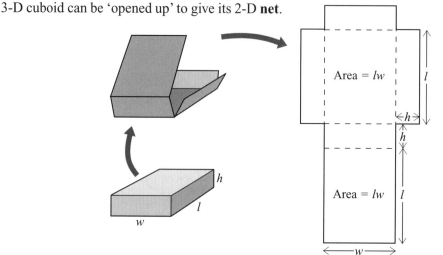

Area = *lw*
l
h
h
Area = *lw*
l
h
l
w

The area of the net is called the **surface area**. For a cuboid with length l, width w and height h, the surface area is given by the formula:

surface area $= 2lw + 2lh + 2wh$

Example 1

The box (cuboid) has a volume of 60 cm^3.
Sketch the net and calculate the surface area of the box.

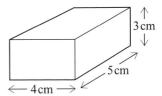

Solution

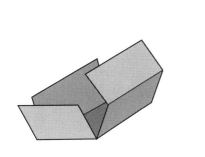

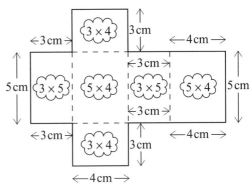

Surface area $= 2 \times (3 \times 5) + 2 \times (3 \times 4) + 2 \times (5 \times 4)$
$= 30 + 24 + 40$
$= 94 \text{ cm}^2$

2 This cuboid also has a volume of 60 cm^3.
Sketch the net and calculate the surface area of the cuboid.

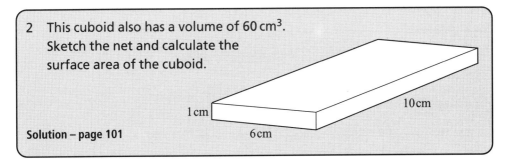

Solution – page 101

A cuboid is an example of a **prism**. A 3-dimensional object is a prism if the area of its base is maintained right through its height to the top. Some examples of prisms are shown below.

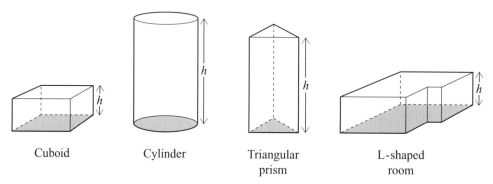

| Cuboid | Cylinder | Triangular prism | L-shaped room |

The volume of a prism is:

volume = base area × height

In the examples above, the base area is shaded and h is the height.

A prism can be 'on its side'.

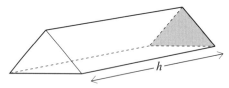

The formula still applies, but 'height' is now a length.

For a cylinder:

volume = area of circle × height of cylinder
$$= \pi r^2 \times h$$

For a triangular prism:

volume = area of triangle × length of prism

Example 2

Calculate the volume of the cylinder:

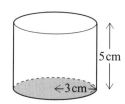

5 cm

←3 cm→

Solution

$$\begin{aligned}
\text{Area of circle} &= \pi r^2 \\
&= \pi \times 3 \times 3 \\
&= 28 \cdot 27 \,\text{cm}^2 \\
\text{Volume of cylinder} &= 28 \cdot 27 \times 5 \\
&= 141 \cdot 4 \,\text{cm}^3 \quad \text{(to 1 d.p.)}
\end{aligned}$$

3　Calculate the volume of this triangular prism.

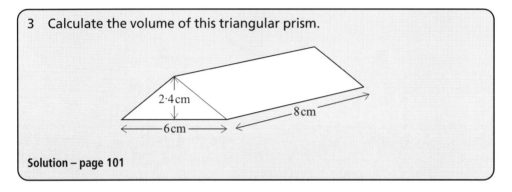

Solution – page 101

Further practice and applications:　*Tin can labels (page 6)*
Crisp boxes (page 15)
Planning permission (page 35)

2.4 Plans and drawings

When a 3-dimensional object is not simple, a drawing can be confusing. Detailed information is often best shown on a **plan** of the object. A plan is the 2-dimensional view of an object when seen from above. An estate agent will sometimes include a plan of a house to give prospective purchasers a clear picture of the layout of the rooms.

Example 1

The ground floor plan of a house is shown below.

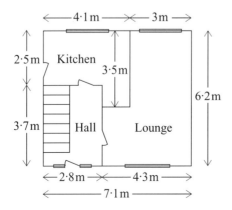

Calculate the area of the lounge.

Solution

Dimensions which are not marked on the plan can be worked out from the measurements given. The plan of the lounge with all the dimensions marked is shown.

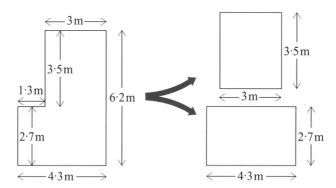

To calculate the area, split the shape into two rectangles.
Area $= (3{\cdot}5 \times 3) + (4{\cdot}3 \times 2{\cdot}7)$
$\quad\quad = 22{\cdot}11\ \text{m}^2$

1 A plumber installing central heating has to calculate the volume of a room to determine the radiator size.
(a) Use the plan in example 1 to calculate the floor area of the kitchen.
(b) The kitchen is 2·4 m high. Calculate the volume of the kitchen.

Solution – page 102

Further practice and applications: *The painter's problem (page 21)*
Landscaping (page 24)
Planning permission (page 35)

2.5 Measuring instruments and levels of accuracy

Many problems involve measuring. For example, when ordering new curtains you must first measure the width and height of the window; when ordering fuel oil you must first measure the dimensions of the container so that you can calculate its capacity; and when sowing barley you must first measure the dimensions of the field to calculate its area.

It is important that you consider carefully how accurate your measurements need to be as well as what measuring instrument is appropriate for the job.

Example 1

A farmer has to measure a field to calculate its perimeter before ordering fencing materials. What measuring instrument might she use?

Solution

She could walk the length and width of the field and count the number of paces it takes. If she then measures her pace, she can calculate the dimensions of the field with reasonable accuracy. She would use a long tape measure to measure, say, 10 paces so that she could calculate the average length of each pace.

She could look at an accurate map of the farm and measure the dimensions from the map. In this case she would use a ruler graduated in millimetres to measure the map as accurately as possible.

Example 2

The length of a rectangle is measured as 7 cm and the width as 4 cm. Both measurements are to the nearest centimetre. The perimeter is 22 cm, but how accurate is this?

Solution

The length is 7 cm to the nearest centimetre. That means it could, in fact, be anything from 6·5 cm to 7·5 cm ($7 \pm 0·5$ cm). Similarly, the width could be anything from 3·5 cm to 4·5cm ($4 \pm 0·5$ cm). The two extremes are:
- *minimum*: the length is really 6·5 cm but was rounded up to 7 cm, and the width is really 3·5 cm but was rounded up to 4 cm;
- *maximum*: the length is really 7·5 cm but was rounded down to 7 cm, and the width is really 4·5 cm but was rounded down to 4 cm.

The possible variation in actual size is shown in the shaded area:

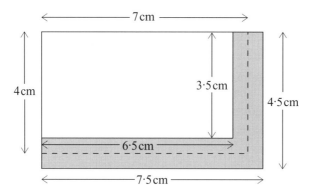

The perimeter can be anything from:
- minimum: $(3\cdot5 + 6\cdot5 + 3\cdot5 + 6\cdot5)\,\text{cm} = 20\,\text{cm}$
- maximum: $(4\cdot5 + 7\cdot5 + 4\cdot5 + 7\cdot5)\,\text{cm} = 24\,\text{cm}$

The perimeter is 22 ± 2 cm. So the perimeter is *not* accurate to the nearest centimetre. You would have to measure the rectangle more accurately if you require greater accuracy in the perimeter.

---

1 (a) The area of the rectangle in example 2 is $7\,\text{cm} \times 4\,\text{cm} = 28\,\text{cm}^2$.
       How accurate is this?
   (b) The dimensions of the rectangle are found to be $7\cdot1$ cm by $4\cdot2$ cm
       when measured to the nearest millimetre. What is the perimeter
       and how accurate is your calculation?

Solution – page 103

The second example illustrates the importance of considering what calculations you are going to do when deciding how accurate your measurements need to be.

Further practice and applications: *Landscaping (page 24)*

3 Handling data

3.1 Conversion of units

It is still common for quantities to be measured in different units. Some trades work in metres while others prefer the old imperial measures of feet and inches; you buy a litre of cola but milk comes in pints; road distances are measured in kilometres on the continent and in miles in Britain. The list of examples goes on. You can appreciate that it is necessary to be able to convert from one system of units to another.

3.1.1 Scales

You can often convert between units of measurement using a **conversion scale**. A tape measure, for example, is often calibrated in inches as well as centimetres, and a car's speedometer gives readings in both miles per hour (m.p.h) and kilometres per hour (km/h).

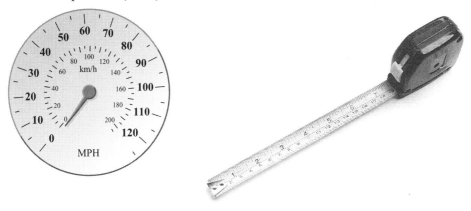

Example 1

Sandra is 5 ft 6 in tall. How tall is she in centimetres?

Solution

There are 12 inches in a foot.
5 ft 6 in is $5 \times 12 + 6 = 66$ inches.
Look up 66 inches on a tape measure.

66 in = 167·6 cm

Sandra is 167·6 cm tall (i.e. 167 cm and 6 mm).
You would probably say that Sandra is 168 cm tall, rounding your answer to the nearest centimetre.

Example 2

The speed limit in towns in Denmark is 50 kilometres per hour.
What speed is this in miles per hour?

Solution

A car speedometer shows
this to be about 31 miles per hour.

31 mph

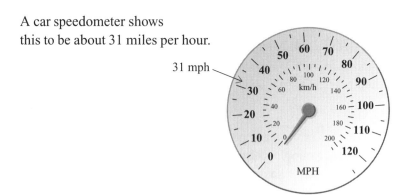

---

1   (a) Use a tape measure to convert 6 ft 1 in to centimetres.
    (b) The distance between Morpeth and Alnwick is 21 miles. Use the
         car speedometer above to convert this to kilometres.

Solution – page 103

3.1.2 Tables

Conversion tables are also used to convert between units.

Table for converting from acres to hectares

Acres	0	1	2	3	4	5	6	7	8	9
0	0·00	0·40	0·81	1·21	1·62	2·02	2·43	2·83	3·24	3·64
10	4·05	4·45	4·86	5·26	5·67	6·07	6·47	6·88	7·28	7·69
20	8·09	8·50	8·90	9·31	9·71	10·12	10·52	10·93	11·33	11·74
30	12·14	12·55	12·95	13·35	13·76	14·16	14·57	14·97	15·38	15·78
40	16·19	16·59	17·00	17·40	17·81	18·21	18·62	19·02	19·42	19·83
50	20·23	20·64	21·04	21·45	21·85	22·26	22·66	23·07	23·47	23·88
60	24·28	24·69	25·09	25·50	25·90	26·30	26·71	27·11	27·52	27·92
70	28·33	28·73	29·14	29·54	29·95	30·35	30·76	31·16	31·57	31·97
80	32·37	32·78	33·18	33·59	33·99	34·40	34·80	35·21	35·61	36·02
90	36·42	36·83	37·23	37·64	38·04	38·45	38·85	39·25	39·66	40·06

Example 3

A manufacturer's instructions recommend that when sowing grass seed you should use 0·6 tonnes of seed per hectare. How many tonnes of seed do you need to sow a 53-acre field?

Solution

The shaded box in the conversion table shows you that
53 acres = 21·45 hectares.
You would need 21·45 × 0·6 = 12·87 tonnes of grass seed.
(The farmer would probably order 13 tonnes.)

> **2** A farmer has a 73-acre field. He has to convert this to hectares. How many hectares is his field?
>
> **Solution – page 103**

3.1.3 Calculation

You can convert between units by **calculation**.

Example 4

The Williams family uses 3 pints of milk each day. On holiday they buy their milk by the litre. What is their weekly consumption in litres?

Solution

In section 2.1 you saw that 1 litre is roughly 2 pints.
A more accurate conversion is:

$$1 \text{ litre} = 1 \cdot 76 \text{ pints} \quad \text{(to 2 d.p.)}$$

The Williams family consumes 3 pints per day, that is
$7 \times 3 = 21$ pints per week.

$$21 \text{ pints} = 21 \div 1 \cdot 76 \text{ litres}$$
$$= 11 \cdot 93 \text{ litres} \quad \text{(to 2 d.p.)}$$
$$\approx 12 \text{ litres}$$

3 (a) What would be your solution to example 4 if you used the rough conversion 1 litre ≈ 2 pints?

   (b) (i) Use the rough conversion, 1 litre ≈ 2 pints to convert 17 litres to pints.

        (ii) Use the accurate conversion 1 litre = 1.76 pints, to convert 17 litres to pints.

   (c) When might you use a rough conversion rather than an accurate one?

Solution – page 103

Further practice and applications: Australia (page 18)
Cycle computer (page 32)

3.2 Data collection

Before carrying out a survey, you first need to *plan*. You need to decide what information is required and what is the best way to obtain the information. There are various ways of collecting data:

- by observation – for example, shopping habits at supermarkets, including transport used, types of trolleys required, which days are busy, and so on;
- by questionnaire – for example, people's views on a proposed sports centre;
- by research – for example, birth rates and populations in different countries;
- by experiment – for example, pulse rates before and after strenuous exercise;
- by a combination of the above.

3.2.1 Questionnaires

All questions in a **questionnaire** must be clear and easy to answer. A small **pilot survey** is usually used to test the questions, which can then be revised as a result of the replies obtained.

The set of all the people within the group you are interested in is called the **population**. However, it is normally too expensive and complicated to survey the whole population, so a **sample** is surveyed. The sample should be picked at random from the population. It needs to be as **representative** as possible of the population, for example, a similar mix of ages, gender, background. The larger a sample, the more reliable the results will be.

When designing a questionnaire, you need to consider the following:
- Have you written a brief and simple explanation of the purpose of the survey? This should encourage the respondent to take the time to answer the questions.
- Are the questions clear and simple to answer and will the answers be easy to analyse? Multi-response questions and tick boxes are both easy to answer and easy to analyse.
- Have you made any prejudgements?
- Have you included any leading questions? A leading question is one which seems to expect a certain answer.
- Have you included any sensitive questions? Some people are sensitive about giving information such as age and weight. This type of question must be written carefully so as to avoid giving offence.
- Have you asked any unnecessary questions? People are less likely to answer the questionnaire if it is too long.

Asking the questions directly, rather than leaving the questionnaire with the respondent to answer and send back later, will receive a much higher number of responses. (30% might be considered a good postal response!) However, you must respect a person's right to refuse to take part in any survey.

---

1   What is wrong with the following questions?
   (a) What is your opinion on care for the mentally ill in the community?
   (b) How old are you?
   (c) In what ways do you think the proposed site for flats for the mentally ill is unsuitable?

   Solution – page 104

An example questionnaire for a survey on mental health care follows.

Make sure the grammar and spelling are correct.

Explain the purpose of the survey.

I am conducting a survey to find out opinions of voters about the proposed supervised flats for the mentally ill in this neighbourhood. Please would you spare a few minutes of your time. The results will be used by the Council's Planning Committee.

1 What age group are you in?

Make sure the categories do not overlap.

    (a) 18–25

    (b) 26–35

    (c) 36–50

    (d) over 50

You can analyse these results to make sure you have a good mix of age and gender.

2 Gender: Male/Female

3 How would you express your opinion about supervised care for the mentally ill in the community?

    (a) Strongly in favour

    (b) In favour

    (c) No opinion

    (d) Against

    (e) Strongly against

Tick-boxes are helpful for easy analysis.

4 Did you know previously of the proposal to build supervised flats for the mentally ill in your neighbourhood?

    Yes/No

5 The proposed site for the flats is in Atherstone Drive (see attached map). What is your opinion about the location?

Do not assume knowledge of the area.

    (a) Suitable

    (b) No opinion

    (c) Not suitable

6 If you think the proposed site is unsuitable, please give your reasons.

An opportunity can be given for respondents to express their views, even though this may be hard to analyse.

Thank you for your co-operation.

Politeness is important.

3.2.2 Data collection sheets

A **data collection sheet** can be used either to collect data directly or to record the data collected using a questionnaire. Before you design a data collection sheet, it is useful to think about how you might want to present your data. This should help you decide how to record the information.

Two examples of data collection sheets are shown here, one for recording the data from the questionnaire on mental health care and one for collecting information on visitors to a sports centre.

Mental Health Survey

> Information is entered here for the first person in the sample. The sheet must be quick to fill in (use a simple code) and easy to extract data from.

Sample	1	2	3	4	5	6	7	8
1 Age	b							
2 Gender	F							
3 Care in the community	e							
4 Previous knowledge	Y							
5 Location	b							

> Multiple sheets can be used depending on size of survey.

Sports centre survey

Transport Used	Total
Car	
Bus	
Bicycle	
Taxi	
Other	

Age and Gender	Male	Total	Female	Total
Under 10				
10–14				
15–19				
20–24				
25 and over				

Further practice and applications: *Food additives (page 9)*
Adventure park (page 11)

3.3. Discrete and grouped data

Data are either descriptive or numeric. The colour of a person's eyes is descriptive; the person's weight, on the other hand, is measured using numbers and is therefore numeric. There are two types of numeric data.

Measurements which can only have *whole number values* are called **discrete data**. The number of eggs in a nest, the number of phone calls received by a fire station during a day and the number of pages in a book are all examples of discrete data. It would not, for instance, be sensible for a fire station to claim to have received six and half phone calls; it would have to be a whole number, say six or seven.

Continuous data depend on measuring accuracy and so cannot be given exact values. For example, the weight of a person is often given to the nearest kilogram. So a person whose weight is given as 55 kg weighs somewhere between 54 kg 500 g and 55 kg 500 g.

---

1 Some of the data below are discrete. Identify the discrete data and the continuous data. For the continuous data, say how accurate the measurements might be.
   (a) the number of cars which pass a particular point during a one-minute time interval
   (b) the volume of milk in a bottle
   (c) the number of children in a family
   (d) the temperature at midnight
   (e) the mark a student achieves in a test

Solution – page 104

Data can be **grouped**.

Example 1

A machine is set up to record the number of vehicles which pass a particular point on a road every five minutes. The results over a four-hour period are:

2, 12, 34, 24, 36, 13, 8, 12, 18, 21, 33, 22, 21, 19, 8, 12, 13, 2, 0, 35, 31, 29, 17, 15, 11, 10, 7, 6, 26, 14, 29, 5, 9, 14, 13, 20, 30, 26, 18, 12, 30, 7, 5, 13, 26, 19, 19, 9.

Group the data and present them in a table.

Solution

Number of cars	Frequency
0–9	12
10–19	19
20–29	10
30–39	7

Although the numbers of cars are discrete data, they have been grouped for convenience.

2 (a) Check that there are 12 data items between 0 and 9 inclusive.
  (b) Why is it convenient to group the data?

Solution – page 104

Further practice and applications: *Adventure park (page 11)*

3.4 Mean, median, mode and range

There are three measures of average: mean, median and mode.

The **range** is the difference between the largest and smallest numbers in a data set.

The **mean** is the average obtained when you add up a set of numbers and then divide by the number of numbers.

Example 1

A student obtained 38%, 56%, 64%, 61%, 87% and 59% in her first six assignments.
(a) What was her mean mark?
(b) What was the range of her marks?

Solution

(a) The total of all her marks was $38 + 56 + 64 + 61 + 87 + 59 = 365$.
  There were 6 assignments.
  The mean was $\dfrac{38 + 56 + 64 + 61 + 87 + 59}{6} = \dfrac{365}{6} = 60 \cdot 833\,333\ldots$
  Her mean mark was 60·8% (rounded to 1 decimal place).
(b) The student's marks ranged from 38% to 87%. So the range was $87 - 38 = 49\%$.

1 (a) Calculate the mean and range for the following two data sets:
       (i) 25, 46, 12, 56, 39
       (ii) 2·9, 8·7, 3·6, 12·1, 4, 1·8, 11·6, 2·9
   (b) The chairman of an angling club has to choose between two
        anglers, Greg and Simon, to fill the last place in a team entering
        a competition. He looks at their performances over the last ten
        matches and notes the following statistics:
        Greg – mean weight of fish caught: 4·7 kg   (range 8·6 kg)
        Simon – mean weight of fish caught: 4·7 kg   (range 2·1 kg)
        Who would you advise him to include in the team? Give your
        reasons.

Solution – page 105

The **median** is the middle number when all the numbers in a data list are
arranged in order of size. (If there are two middle numbers then 'split the
difference'.)

Example 2

The student in example 1 obtained 38%, 56%, 64%, 61%, 87% and
59% in her first six assignments. What was her median mark?

Solution

The six marks arranged in order were: 38, 56, **59**, **61**, 64, 87
In this case there are two middle numbers, 59 and 61. The number
half-way between these two is 60, so the median is 60%.

The **mode** is the data item which occurs most frequently. If there is no repetition
of numbers in a data list, then there is no mode. (In the example above there is no
repetition of data so there is no mode.)

Example 3

Another student achieved these marks in his first nine assignments:
23%, 48%, 44%, 61%, 72%, 61%, 54%, 44%, 61%
Calculate the mean, median, mode and range.

Solution

Mean: $$\frac{23+48+44+61+72+61+54+44+61}{9} = \frac{468}{9}$$
$$= 52\%$$

Median: 23, 44, 44, 48, **54**, 61, 61, 61, 72
The median is 54%.

Mode: In the list above it is easy to see that the mark '61%' has occurred three times. This is more often than any other mark, so the mode is 61%.

Range: $72 - 23 = 49\%$

---

2 In a small business, the managing director has a salary of £35 000 and the production manager has a salary of £25 000. The salaries of five members of staff are £12 000, £14 500, £15 500, £17 000 and £19 000, while a further four members of staff each earn £13 500.

(a) Find the mean, median and mode of the salaries.

(b) All staff negotiate for a pay rise with the board of directors. Explain why, if the average salary is to be used as a basis for negotiation, it is in the board's interest to use the mean, whereas it is in the staff's interest to use the mode.

Solution – page 105

Further practice and applications: *Adventure park (page 11)*
House prices (page 27)
Relative business (page 29)

3.5 Graphs

Graphs are commonly used in mathematics to present a relationship between two (or more) sets of data. Sometimes, however, graphs are used to *misrepresent* a relationship and you need to be aware of how this can happen.

Example 1

The table shows how a firm's profits have increased over a five year period.

Year	1989	1990	1991	1992	1993
Profit	£10 000	£10 100	£10 200	£10 400	£10 800

Explain how the **line graph** below misrepresents the relationship between profit and year.

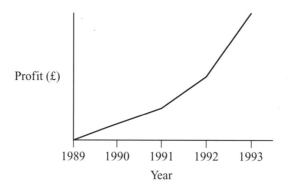

Solution

The graph gives the impression of a dramatic increase in profit year on year. The lack of scale on the 'profit' axis makes it impossible to interpret the graph. The true picture is very different. Look again at the graph when the vertical axis starts at zero.

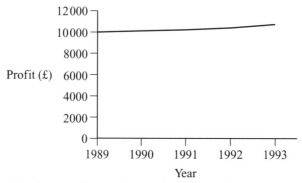

The increase in profit is quite modest in reality.

This type of misrepresentation is common and could, for example, be used to persuade people to invest in a company. Starting at zero is not really sensible either as the data are now concentrated into a very narrow range on the scale. A graph such as the one below is appropriate.

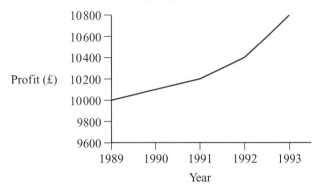

It is important to know how to construct graphs which present data in a way which gives a true picture. Only when you do this are you likely to notice when others are deliberately misrepresenting data.

- Choose **axes** to show data to the best effect. In the example, the profit depends on the year. Profit is the **dependent** variable and time the **independent** variable. Always display the independent variable (often 'time') along the x-axis.
- Put clear **labels** on your axes.
- Select a sensible **scale** for your axes. It is not necessary to start scales at zero. Your scale should allow important features of the data to be displayed effectively.

More than one line graph can be constructed on the same axes. This allows comparisons to be made.

---

1   A company which owns two shops is experiencing financial difficulties and has decided to sell one of the shops. The company's managing director looks at last year's quarterly figures for each shop.

	1st quarter	2nd quarter	3rd quarter	4th quarter
Shop A's profit	£2312	£3305	£3110	£2100
Shop B's profit	£1050	£1255	£3115	£4325

Draw line graphs showing both sets of figures on the same axes. Compare the graphs and recommend a shop to be closed.

Solution – page 106

Further practice and applications: *Relative business (page 29)*

3.6 Pictograms, bar charts and pie charts

3.6.1 Pictograms

Statistical diagrams are used to give a reader a visual representation of data. The simplest type of diagram is a pictogram and this is the type of diagram commonly used by young children to display information.

How do you come to school in the morning?

By car	👤 👤 👤 👤 👤 👤
By school bus	👤 👤 👤 👤 👤 👤 👤 👤
On a bike	👤
On foot	👤 👤 👤 👤 👤

You will find more sophisticated pictograms in magazines and newspapers. When drawn by a graphic artist, a pictogram can be very effective and command the attention of a reader. Their disadvantages are that they are difficult to construct to a professional standard and the information given often lacks detail.

3.6.2 Bar charts

The information from two or more bar charts is often combined and displayed on a single compound bar chart. This helps convey the differences in the data set.

Example 1

Information on how the membership of a local table tennis club has changed over the last few years is shown in the table below.

Year	1990	1991	1992	1993	1994
Boys	7	9	12	10	10
Girls	3	5	9	12	14

Illustrate this information on a bar chart.

Solution

Two possible solutions are given below:

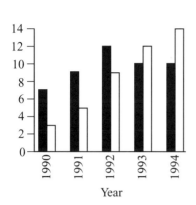 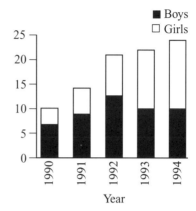

> 1 Which of the two bar charts do you think is most effective? List any advantages or disadvantages that one has compared with the other.
>
> **Solution – page 106**

3.6.3 Pie charts

Pie charts are very useful for looking at percentages.

You often have the choice of drawing a pie chart or a bar chart. You have to decide which conveys the information most effectively.

Example 2

As part of an investigation into the effect food additives have on children's behaviour, Tony, an assistant on the research project, collected the following information from 250 questionnaires sent to parents:

Was your child's behaviour generally:

worse than normal	120
the same as normal	85
better than normal	45

Draw a pie chart to display this information.

Solution

There were 250 responses to the questionnaire.

45 children behaved better than normal. This is $\frac{45}{250} = 18\%$ of the sample. They will be represented by a sector (slice of pie chart) with angle:

18% of $360° = 0·18 \times 360°$
$\qquad\qquad\quad = 64·8°$

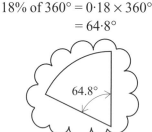

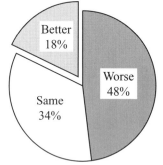

2 (a) Show the calculations needed to work out the angles for the other two sectors.
   (b) Do you think a bar chart could have been used to display the information just as effectively?

Solution – page 106

3.6.4 Computer-generated charts

Computers produce excellent statistical charts. Information stored on a database or spreadsheet can be turned into a statistical chart at the touch of a button. Using a computer you can quickly call up a variety of possible displays, but it is still your decision which one to choose. The computer cannot think for you, it can only carry out the calculations accurately. You still have to decide which chart conveys the information more effectively.

Example 3

Information on how the membership of the local table tennis club in example 1 has changed over the last few years is shown in the table below.

Year	1990	1991	1992	1993	1994
Boys	7	9	12	10	10
Girls	3	5	9	12	14
Total	10	14	21	22	24

Use a computer to produce a variety of different displays showing how the membership has changed over the years.

Solution

The following diagrams were produced using the spreadsheet program EXCEL.

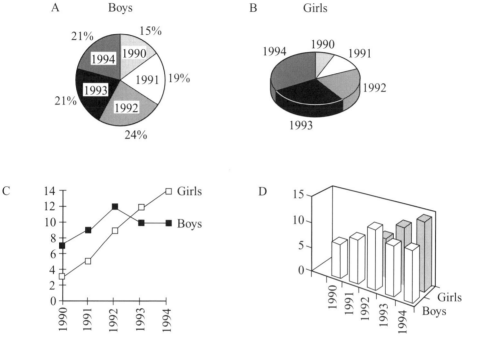

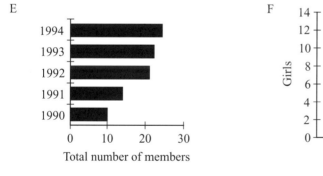

```
3   Which of the diagrams do you think are effective? Which are not so
    effective? Give reasons.
Solution – page 107
```

Further practice and applications: *Adventure park (page 11)*
Relative business (page 29)

D Solutions (Core skill techniques)

1 Number

1.1 Fractions, decimals, percentages and ratios

1.1.1 Fractions

1. (a) $\overset{\div 2}{\overbrace{}}$ $\frac{6}{16} = \frac{3}{8}$ $\underset{\div 2}{\underbrace{}}$ 　(b) $\overset{\div 3}{\overbrace{}}$ $\frac{9}{24} = \frac{3}{8}$ $\underset{\div 3}{\underbrace{}}$ 　(c) $\overset{\div 5}{\overbrace{}}$ $\frac{15}{40} = \frac{3}{8}$ $\underset{\div 5}{\underbrace{}}$

   (d) $\overset{\div 5}{\overbrace{}}$ $\frac{10}{25} = \frac{2}{5}$ $\underset{\div 5}{\underbrace{}}$ 　(e) $\overset{\div 10}{\overbrace{}}$ $\frac{30}{80} = \frac{3}{8}$ $\underset{\div 10}{\underbrace{}}$ 　(f) $\overset{\div 10}{\overbrace{}}\overset{\div 8}{\overbrace{}}$ $\frac{240}{640} = \frac{24}{64} = \frac{3}{8}$ $\underset{\div 10}{\underbrace{}}\underset{\div 8}{\underbrace{}}$

   $\frac{10}{25}$ is the only one *not* equivalent to $\frac{3}{8}$.

2. (a) $\frac{3}{4} + \frac{2}{5} = \frac{15}{20} + \frac{8}{20} = \frac{23}{20} = 1\frac{3}{20}$
   (b) $\frac{2}{3} + \frac{4}{5} = \frac{10}{15} + \frac{12}{15} = \frac{22}{15} = 1\frac{7}{15}$
   (c) $\frac{5}{8} - \frac{1}{3} = \frac{15}{24} - \frac{8}{24} = \frac{7}{24}$

3. (a) $\frac{1}{2} = 0\cdot5$ 　　　(b) $\frac{3}{4} = 0\cdot75$ 　　　(c) $\frac{5}{8} = 0\cdot625$
   (d) $\frac{7}{16} = 0\cdot4375$ 　(e) $\frac{35}{100} = 0\cdot35$ 　(f) $\frac{3}{7} = 0\cdot428\,571\,42...$

   You should know results such as $\frac{1}{2} = 0\cdot5$ and $\frac{3}{4} = 0\cdot75$.
   You should be able to work out $35 \div 100$ in your head.
   You probably need to use a calculator to work out $3 \div 7$ to change a
   fraction such as $\frac{3}{7} = 0\cdot428\,57...$

4. (a) (i) $0\cdot384\,326 = 0\cdot4$ 　(to 1 d.p.) 　　The 3 is rounded up to 4
   　　　　　　　　　　　　　　　　　　　because the next digit, 8, is
   　　　　　　　　　　　　　　　　　　　greater than 5 and so the
   　　　　　　　　　　　　　　　　　　　decimal is nearer 0·4 than 0·3.

   　　(ii) $0\cdot384\,326 = 0\cdot38$ 　(to 2 d.p.) 　　The 8 is not rounded up to 9
   　　　　　　　　　　　　　　　　　　　because the next digit, 4, is less
   　　　　　　　　　　　　　　　　　　　than 5 and so the decimal is
   　　　　　　　　　　　　　　　　　　　nearer 0·38 than 0·39.

   　　(iii) $0\cdot384\,326 = 0\cdot384$ 　(to 3 d.p.) 　　The 4 is not rounded up to 5
   　　　　　　　　　　　　　　　　　　　because the next digit, 3, is less
   　　　　　　　　　　　　　　　　　　　than 5 and so the decimal is
   　　　　　　　　　　　　　　　　　　　nearer 0·384 than 0·385.

   (b) (i) $0\cdot5$ 　(to 1 d.p.) 　(ii) $0\cdot55$ 　(to 2 d.p.) 　(iii) $0\cdot546$ 　(to 3 d.p.)

(c) (i) 0·3 (to 1 d.p.) (ii) 0·30 (to 2 d.p.) (iii) 0·296 (to 3 d.p.)

5 (a) 25% of £37·60 = 0·25 × 37·6

$0·25 × 37·6 = 9·4$

   = £9·40

(b) 17·5% of £19·99 = 0·175 × 19·99

   = £3·50

$0·175 × 19·99 = 3·498\ 25$
which is rounded to 3·50 to 2 d.p.

6 (a) $\frac{1}{2} = 0·5 = 50\%$ (b) $\frac{3}{4} = 0·75 = 75\%$

   (c) $\frac{5}{8} = 0·625 = 62·5\%$ (d) $\frac{7}{16} = 0·4375 = 43·8\%$

   (e) $\frac{3}{7} = 0·428\ 571\ 42... = 42·9\%$ (f) $\frac{135}{600} = 0·225 = 22·5\%$

   (Answers are rounded to one decimal place.)

7 Between them, Alan and Beth would have worked 16 hours. As Alan would have worked 6 of these, he would be entitled to $\frac{6}{16}$ of the money. But $\frac{6}{16}$ and $\frac{3}{8}$ are equivalent fractions so his share is the same.

8 (a)   3 : 5

   × 15 ↓   ↓ × 15

         45 : 75

   (b) The multiplier is 15 because they are paid £15 per hour. The final ratio 45 : 75 shows Alan's share (£45) and Beth's share (£75) of the money.

   (c) Between them they worked 25 hours. Alan worked 15 of these hours so his share is $\frac{15}{25}$ of the the £360.
   To calculate Alan's share, first work out $\frac{1}{25}$ of £360.

   $$\frac{1}{25} \times £360 = £360 \div 25$$
   $$= £14·40$$

   $$\frac{15}{25} \times £360 = 15 \times £14·4$$
   $$= £216$$

   so Alan's share is £216. (Beth receives £360 − £216 = £144.)
   (Note that $\frac{15}{25} = \frac{3}{5}$, so you could have calculated $\frac{3}{5}$ of £360.)

1.2 Probability descriptions

1 (a) (i) 3 ÷ 20 = 0·15   (ii) 0·15 = 15%

   (b) (i) $\frac{3}{15}$ (ii) 3 ÷ 15 = 0·2   (iii) 0·2 = 20%

   (c)   (i)(ii)

   0   ↓↓ $\frac{1}{2}$ 1

   Probability line

   (d) The first production line is the more reliable as a firework from this production line is less likely to fail.

1.3 Negative numbers

1   (a) $4 + {}^-2 = 4 - 2$
           $= 2$

  (b) $15 + {}^-6 = 15 - 6$
            $= 9$

  (c) ${}^-5 + {}^-3 = {}^-5 - 3$
            $= {}^-8$

  (d) $5 + {}^-5 = 5 - 5$
          $= 0$

  (e) $5 + {}^-8 = 5 - 8$
          $= {}^-3$

  (f) $5 + {}^-33 = 5 - 33$
          $= {}^-28$

2   (a) $4 - {}^-2 = 4 + 2$
           $= 6$

  (b) $15 - {}^-6 = 15 + 6$
           $= 21$

  (c) ${}^-5 - {}^-3 = {}^-5 + 3$
           $= {}^-2$

  (d) ${}^-5 - {}^-5 = {}^-5 + 5$
          $= 0$

  (e) ${}^-5 - {}^-8 = {}^-5 + 8$
          $= 3$

  (f) $5 - {}^-33 = 5 + 33$
          $= 38$

1.4 Estimation, prediction and checking procedures

1   (a) 85% of $£260 = 0{\cdot}85 \times £260$
              $= £221$

  (b) $£2{\cdot}66 + £78{\cdot}99 + £43 + £123{\cdot}5 = £248{\cdot}15$

    An alternative check would be to subtract each of the numbers from £248·15:

    $£248{\cdot}15 - £123{\cdot}50 - £43 - £78{\cdot}99 - £2{\cdot}66 = 0$

2   $7 \times £34{\cdot}86 = £244{\cdot}02$

  Note that in this case the check shows the result to be incorrect. The answer should be £244. The error occurred because the result of the division, 34·857 142…, was rounded up to 34·86. That was a mistake in this context. In fact, each worker should only receive £34·85. As $7 \times £34{\cdot}85 = £243{\cdot}95$, there will be 5p left. This could be given to charity. It cannot be split 7 ways!

3   (a) Round 279 up to 300 and 213 down to 200.

    $300 \times 200 = 60\,000$

    So 279×213 is about 60 000.

    In fact $279 \times 213 = 59\,427$.

  (b) Round 392 up to 400 and 48 up to 50.

    $400 \div 50 = 8$

    So $392 \div 48$ is about 8.

    In fact $392 \div 48 = 8{\cdot}1666…$

  (c) Round 5·78 up to 6 and 18·87 up to 20.

    $6 \times 20 = 120$

    So $5{\cdot}78 \times 18{\cdot}87$ is about 120.

    In fact $5{\cdot}78 \times 18{\cdot}87 = 109{\cdot}0686$.

4   (a) The correct calculation is $1300 \div 30$.
       (In this case the error is the common mistake of the division being the wrong way around.)
    (b) $1300 \div 30 = 43 \cdot 333\ldots$
       She types just over 43 words per minute. (Although it is slightly slower than expected, the result is not unreasonable.)

1.5 Formulas in words and symbols

1   $p = 3q - 5r$
$$= 3 \times q - 5 \times r$$
$$= 3 \times 9 - 5 \times 4$$
$$= 27 - 20$$
$$= 7$$

2   $p = 3q^2 - 5r$
$$= 3 \times q \times q - 5 \times r$$
$$= 3 \times 6 \times 6 - 5 \times 4$$
$$= 108 - 20$$
$$= 88$$

2 Shape, space and measure

2.1 Units of measurement

1   (a) (i) 8 stone 5 pound $= 8 \times 14 + 5$
$$= 117 \text{ pounds}$$
       (ii) 117 pounds is approximately $117 \div 2 \cdot 2 = 53 \text{ kg}$.
    (b) 1200 litres is approximately $1200 \times 0 \cdot 22 = 264$ gallons.
    (c) 8 feet 6 inches is approximately:
       $8 \times 30 + 6 \times 2 \cdot 5 = 255$ centimetres
$$= 2 \cdot 55 \text{ metres}$$
    (d) 5 miles is approximately $5 \times 1600 = 8000$ metres
$$= 8 \text{ km}$$

2.2 2-dimensional problems – perimeter and area

1 (a) Not all the dimensions are shown. Two are missing. However, these
are easy to calculate and are shown on the diagram.

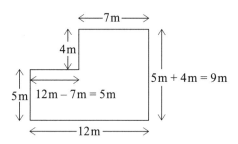

Perimeter $= (5 + 5 + 4 + 7 + 9 + 12)\,m$

$\qquad = 42\,m$

(b) You can think of this shape as these
two rectangles stuck together:

Area $= (12 \times 5) + (7 \times 4)$

$\qquad = 60 + 28$

$\qquad = 88\,m^2$ (square metres)

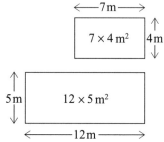

2 If you turn the triangle around it looks like this:
You can now see that the base is 4·2 cm
and the height is 2·4 cm.

Area $= \frac{1}{2}$ (base $\times$ height)

$\qquad = \frac{1}{2}\,(4\cdot2 \times 2\cdot4)$

$\qquad = 5\cdot04\,cm^2$

Note that the 3·6 cm length is not used in calculating the area.

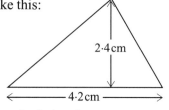

3 The radius is 3 m so the diameter is $2 \times 3 = 6\,m$.

$\qquad c = \pi \times d$

$\qquad\quad = \pi \times 6$

$\qquad\quad = 18\cdot849\,55 \ldots$

The circumference is 18·85 m (to the nearest cm).

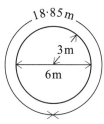

4 (a) Circumference of a full circle with diameter 10 m is $\pi \times 10 = 31\cdot4\,m$.

The curved part of the semicircle will
be $31\cdot4 \div 2 = 15\cdot7\,m$.

The perimeter is therefore

$10 + 15\cdot7 = 25\cdot7\,m$ (to 1 d.p.).

(b) The circle has diameter 10 m and so has radius 5 m. The area of a full circle with radius 5 m is $\pi \times 5 \times 5 = 78\cdot54\,\text{m}^2$ so the area of the semicircle is $78\cdot54 \div 2 = 39\cdot27\,\text{m}^2$ (to 2 d.p.).

2.3 3-dimensional problems – volumes

1   (a) For the first cuboid: width $= 3$ cm; height $= 2$ cm; depth $= 6$ cm

   volume $=$ width $\times$ height $\times$ depth

$$= 3 \times 2 \times 6$$
$$= 36\,\text{cm}^3$$

   For the second cuboid: width $= 3$ cm; height $= 4$ cm; depth $= 3$ cm

   volume $=$ width $\times$ height $\times$ depth

$$= 3 \times 4 \times 3$$
$$= 36\,\text{cm}^3$$

   (b) Volume $= 8\cdot7 \times 5\cdot2 \times 12\cdot5$

$$= 565\cdot5\,\text{m}^3$$

2

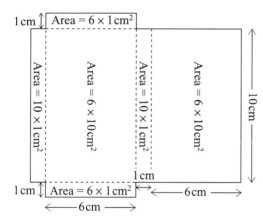

Surface area $= 2 \times (6 \times 10) + 2 \times (6 \times 1) + 2 \times (10 \times 1)$

$$= 120 + 12 + 20$$
$$= 152\,\text{cm}^2$$

3   Area of triangle $= \frac{1}{2} \times$ base $\times$ height

$$= 0\cdot5 \times 6 \times 2\cdot4$$
$$= 7\cdot2\,\text{cm}^2$$

   Volume of prism $=$ area of triangle $\times$ length of prism

$$= 7\cdot2 \times 8$$
$$= 57\cdot6\,\text{cm}^3$$

2.4 Plans and drawings

1 (a)

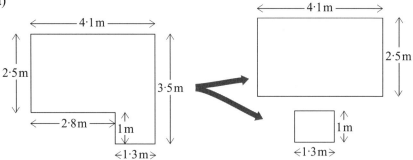

The plan of the kitchen is shown above. Split the shape into two rectangles to calculate the area.

$$\text{Area} = (4 \cdot 1 \times 2 \cdot 5) + (1 \cdot 3 \times 1)$$
$$= 11 \cdot 55 \, \text{m}^2$$

(b) The room is a prism with base area $11 \cdot 55 \, \text{m}^2$ and height $2 \cdot 4 \, \text{m}$.

$$\text{Volume} = 11 \cdot 55 \times 2 \cdot 4$$
$$= 27 \cdot 72 \, \text{m}^3$$

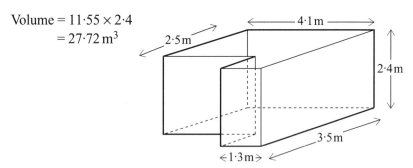

Or: consider the room to be two cuboids:

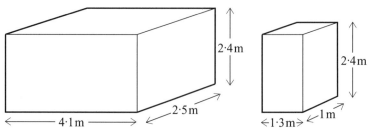

$$\text{Volume} = (4 \cdot 1 \times 2 \cdot 5 \times 2 \cdot 4) + (1 \cdot 3 \times 1 \times 2 \cdot 4)$$
$$= 27 \cdot 72 \, \text{m}^3$$

2.5 Measuring instruments and levels of accuracy

1. (a) Minimum area: $6·5\,\text{cm} \times 3·5\,\text{cm} = 22·75\,\text{cm}^2$
    Maximum area: $7·5\,\text{cm} \times 4·5\,\text{cm} = 33·75\,\text{cm}^2$
    The area is not calculated very accurately!
   (b) The dimensions are $7·1 \pm 0·05\,\text{cm}$ by $4·2 \pm 0·05\,\text{cm}$.
    Minimum perimeter: $(7·05 + 4·15 + 7·05 + 4·15)\,\text{cm} = 22·4\,\text{cm}$
    Maximum perimeter: $(7·15 + 4·25 + 7·15 + 4·25)\,\text{cm} = 22·8\,\text{cm}$
    The perimeter is $22·6 \pm 0·2\,\text{cm}$.

3 Handling data

3.1 Conversion of units

1. (a) 1 foot = 12 inches so 6ft 1in = $6 \times 12 + 1$
    $= 72 + 1$
    $= 73$ inches

   A tape measure shows this to be 185·4 cm.
   (b) A car speedometer shows that 21 miles per hour is equivalent to between 33 and 34 kilometres per hour.
    21 miles is therefore between 33 and 34 kilometres.

2. The table shows that 73 acres is 29·54 hectares.

3. (a) 21 pints $\approx 21 \div 2$ Compare this with the more
    $\approx 10·5$ litres   accurate value of 11·93 litres.
   (b) (i) 17 litres $\approx 17 \times 2$
        ≈ 34 pints
    (ii) 17 litres $= 17 \times 1·76$ pints   The accurate conversion gives
        $= 29·92$ pints   just under 30 pints compared to
                        34 pints using the rough conversion.
   (c) A rough conversion can be carried out easily in your head. You would use a calculator for an accurate conversion. A rough mental conversion is often useful.

3.2 Data collection

1 (a) There is not sufficient guidance in this question. Some respondents may not know how to respond and feel threatened, while others may use the freedom offered to give a great variety of responses. The grouping of these responses for analysis may be extremely difficult. A multi-response question will help to overcome these problems. See question 3 of the example questionnaire for an alternative question.

(b) This may be a sensitive question for many people. The difficulty can be overcome by a wide banding of age groups. See question 1 of the example questionnaire.

(c) This implies that the site is unsuitable and so influences the respondent's reply. See question 5 of the example questionnaire for a more suitable question.

3.3 Discrete and grouped data

1 (a) The number of cars is discrete data.

(b) The volume of milk in a bottle is continuous data and might be measured to the nearest centilitre (cl) or the nearest millilitre (ml) depending on the accuracy expected.

(c) The number of children in a family is discrete data.

(d) The temperature at midnight is continuous data and would probably be measured to the nearest degree.

(e) A mark (as opposed to a grade) is a number, for example 16 out of 25. This would be discrete data.

2 (a) The data items are: 2, 8, 8, 2, 0, 7, 6, 5, 9, 7, 5, 9.

(b) It is convenient because it helps you interpret the data. The numbers in the list are jumbled up and therefore difficult to interpret. By grouping them in a table it is, for example, clear that between 10 and 19 vehicles is most frequent and that it is relatively unusual for there to be 30 or more vehicles during a five-minute interval. These conclusions would be difficult to reach from the original list.

3.4 Mean, median, mode and range

1 (a) (i) Mean = sum of all the numbers divided by the number of numbers

$$= \frac{25 + 46 + 12 + 56 + 39}{5}$$

$$= \frac{178}{5}$$

$$= 35 \cdot 6$$

Range = largest − smallest

$$= 56 - 12$$

$$= 44$$

(ii) Mean $= \dfrac{2 \cdot 9 + 8 \cdot 7 + 3 \cdot 6 + 12 \cdot 1 + 4 + 1 \cdot 8 + 11 \cdot 6 + 2 \cdot 9}{8}$

$$= \frac{47 \cdot 6}{8}$$

$$= 5 \cdot 95$$

Range $= 12 \cdot 1 - 1 \cdot 8$

$$= 10 \cdot 3$$

(b) Greg and Simon both have the same mean, but there is a considerable difference in the ranges. These statistics suggest that Greg, whose range is greater, is perhaps more inclined to experiment. Sometimes it pays off with a big catch and sometimes he catches very little. Simon rarely records a big catch, but he can always be relied on to contribute a reasonable catch to the team total. The chairman has to make a difficult decision. His decision may be influenced by the past performance of the other teams in the competition.

2 (a) Mean: There are eleven staff altogether. Their total salary is £192 000 (i.e. 35 000 + 25 000 + 12 000 + 14 500 + 15 500 + 17 000 + 19 000 + 13 500 + 13 500 + 13 500 + 13 500).

$$\text{Mean} = \frac{192\,000}{11} = £17\,455$$

Median: The eleven salaries arranged in order are:

12 000, 13 500, 13 500, 13 500, 13 500, **14 500**, 15 500, 17 000, 19 000, 25 000, 35 000

The middle number is £14 500 so this is the median.

Mode: The most frequent salary is £13 500. This is the mode.

(b) The mean is the highest of the three averages. The board of directors could use it to argue that, on average, the staff are well paid and that a large increase is not necessary.

The mode is the lowest of the three averages. The staff could use this to argue that, on average, the staff are not well paid and that a large increase is justified.

3.5 Graphs

1

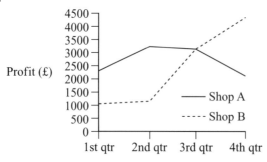

Although shop A has made greater overall profit for the year, shop B appears to be on an upward trend and looks as though it could give a greater return next year. The profits of shop A are decreasing and it may not be so profitable next year. Shop A should be closed.

3.6 Pictograms, bar charts and pie charts

1   The chart on the left highlights how the number of boys compares with the number of girls. Girls started off as a minority. They are now the majority group. Although this is also seen in the other chart, the comparison is not so easy to make.

The chart on the right highlights how the overall numbers have changed over the years as well as giving information on the numbers of boys and girls in the club.

2   (a) Worse than normal: $\dfrac{120}{250} \times 360° = 172\cdot8°$

The same as normal: $\dfrac{85}{250} \times 360° = 122\cdot4°$

(b) This bar chart also shows the responses to the questionnaire. The advantage of a bar chart is that the reader can read off the totals from the scale on the vertical axis.

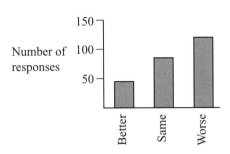

The advantage of the pie chart is that it is more visually attractive and demands little effort from the reader to understand the information it gives. The pie chart shows the percentages, so you can see, for example, that almost 50% of parents said that their child behaved worse than usual.

3 A This is an effective pie chart of a conventional design. However, it does not give much useful information apart from when the membership was highest or lowest. The total membership for the 5 years does not have any meaning, so these percentages are not very useful.

B The three-dimensional quality of this pie chart is very effective but leaves little room for information. Note the lack of percentages. As for A, this pie chart only gives limited information.

C This line graph is an alternative to the compound bar chart in example 1. It shows the comparative trends in the boy/girl membership very effectively.

D This three-dimensional bar chart is visually attractive, but note how the results for the girls in 1990 and 1991 are hidden.

E You often see a bar chart on its side like this. It is an alternative to the usual vertical bar chart.

F This bar chart is nonsense. Unfortunately, programs like EXCEL will allow you to produce graphs like this because the computer cannot think intelligently. It is important that you consider carefully whether or not a graph is sensible.